# ORGANIZATION 2000

# ORGANIZATION 2 0 0 0

## THE ESSENTIAL GUIDE FOR COMPANIES AND TEAMS IN THE NEW ECONOMY

## LESLIE BENDALY

HarperBusiness
HarperCollins*PublishersLtd*

http://www.harpercollins.com/canada

First edition

Canadian Cataloguing in Publication Data

Bendaly, Leslie
Organization 2000 : the essential guide for companies and teams
in the new economy

"A HarperBusiness book"
ISBN 0-00-255428-3

1. Organizational change.    2. Organizational effectiveness.    I. Title.

HD58.8.B45 1996    658.4′062    C96-930732-2

96 97 98 99 ❖ HC 10 9 8 7 6 5 4 3 2 1

Printed and bound in the United States

*For Elie*

# TABLE OF CONTENTS

# PREFACE

In an earlier book, *Strength In Numbers*, I expressed concern that the Achilles' heel of most organizations is that they do not apply what they already know. The concern has not lessened. Many organizations are not sufficiently fit to thrive in the new economy in spite of having restructured and reengineered. Although companies must more than ever before look outside for information, they must start to look more within for answers. Reflection is essential. The faster the world changes, the fewer are the similarities of the experiences of organizations. Each organization must create its own recipe for thriving in the new economy. There is an urgent need to understand the new economy and for swift action to create organizations that work in concert with it. This book is aimed at increasing the understanding of the requirements of the new organization and to provide the information needed to take the essential steps.

*Leslie Bendaly*
*Toronto 1996*

# ACKNOWLEDGMENTS

Innumerable clients and colleagues have contributed directly or indirectly to the creation of the knowledge that is packaged in this book.

I am particularly appreciative of HarperCollins editor Don Loney who brings out the best in books and the best in people; Dr. Yassin Sankar whose extensive work on the value-based organization is a marvelous resource and whose teaching at Dalhousie is preparing members of the next generation of leaders to balance ethics and the bottom line; Peter Beggs for the energy, time and enthusiasm that created an IBM case example of the challenges of the virtual team; my teammate Neda Hadjis who provides indispensable support and is always there to catch whatever might be falling; and my team at home — Elie, Nicole and Chip — who give me energy and challenge my thinking.

# Introduction

# THE ORGANIZATION AS PILGRIM

## UP CLOSE AND PERSONAL — A DISTORTED VIEW

Organizations and institutions are reeling under the forces of frenetic change that they fervently hope will carry them into, and eventually set them down gently in, the new economy. Personal careers and livelihoods, as well as the life of the organization itself, are at stake. It is inevitable that many who are caught up in the struggle are subjectively focused on change as it affects the individual and the organization, and so they miss seeing the bigger picture altogether. The bigger picture displays the pattern of the new economic world order, over which is imposed the pattern of the organization. Standing back and reflecting on the whole reveals whether the patterns are congruent, whether the organization that is being reshaped will be compatible with the new economy.

In exploring that larger picture of the new economy and the organization that will comfortably mesh with it, several key words and phrases will frequently be used. Language quickly takes on different spins for people in different organizations; here is a short glossary.

## The Transition

*The transition is the period of time and those events that link the decline of the industrial-based economy and the rise of the new economy.*

There have been many transitions in our history, each characterized by dramatic change. These transitions are the naturally occurring chaos that emerges to renew a decaying status quo. We cannot, nor would we want to, halt these transitions, although the experience, if not well handled, can be traumatic.

In pinpointing the most significant transitions of the past, historians and economists generally agree that there are major transitions like ours approximately every 200 years. These transitions shift economic structures and culture, including norms of behavior and values.

The transition from a rural-centered society to an urban society, for example, took place in the 1300s. It changed where people lived and how they lived. A new society emerged. One of the changes that powerfully influenced the shape of the new society was the emergence of the city university. This source of power and growth had been previously controlled by monks in remote monasteries. Now, learning and culture had become more accessible.

The Industrial Revolution presents more obvious parallels to our present experience. It was sparked, as are all transitions, by a confluence of various happenings, but the trigger was James Watt's steam engine in 1776. Steam power restructured society into capitalists and workers; changed where people worked and how; changed education systems; and gave birth to a new political philosophy — communism.

A variation of each of these changes, and more, is being played out in our modern transition. The length of the previous transition phases is usually rounded off to 50 years. When ours began is a matter of debate. Certainly, different catalysts are suggested. The first is the computer. The Eniac, the huge, room-sized computer, opened the door (a crack at least) to the information society in 1945. If that were the official beginning, then we should be through the transition — which we are not. Estimated dates of when the present transition will draw to a close range from 2000 to 2020.

In *Post-Capitalist Society*, Peter Drucker suggests the catalyst was the post-World War II American GI *Bill of Rights*, which enabled veterans to attend university. Here he sees the beginning of the shift to the knowledge society.

Whatever the catalyst, perhaps the first real evidence was the employment statistics of the early 1970s that indicated for the first time that white-collar jobs outnumbered blue-collar jobs. Regardless of when the current transition started, we know we are still in it and we need flexibility, energy and vigilance to complete it.

## Knowledge in the New Economy
*Knowledge is the productive application of information.*
Data is incoherent bits. It may be in the form of numbers, words, sounds and images. Information is data arranged coherently so as to have meaning. Information becomes knowledge when it is applied.

## The New Economy
*The new economy is driven by the new basic resource — knowledge.*
When we first began talking about the new economy, it was often described as moving from a manufacturing base to an information and services economy. Skeptics who had not been given enough information scoffed: "You're trying to tell me we aren't going to produce goods any more?" Of course not, but fewer people are employed in the production of goods. Employment figures in manufacturing have drastically decreased and productivity has increased. This increase is due to some extent to workers carrying heavier loads. But for the most part, it is the result of technology allowing us to do more with less.

For years, North American workers were admonished for their low productivity figures compared to those of Japan. One of the major reasons for the huge difference in productivity numbers was that Japan, without a big enough work force to fill its needs, pushed technology much earlier than North America did. In the new economy, technology will handle most of the routine manual information processing and clerical work.

Spin-off businesses created by technology will continue to grow exponentially, many of them becoming more important than the original core business. American Airlines' automated reservations system, Sabre, which they sell to other airlines, now earns much more income than their core business, which is providing air service.

What differentiates the new economy, however, is more than simply employment being generated by the information and services industry. In the new economy, knowledge is the basic resource. Wealth is created by the application of knowledge rather than by labor, and an organization's opportunities for growth lie in becoming a knowledge business. Stan Davis and Jim Botkin, in *The Monster Under the Bed*, note that a knowledge business is "One whose greatest value is derived from the knowledge that has become an intrinsic part of its offering to the market place."

The most important contribution to the business and the economy will be made by the knowledge workers.

## Knowledge Workers

*Knowledge workers use their knowledge to produce products and services.*

The quality of knowledge workers within an organization will determine the quality of the knowledge business. We are not certain yet of the makeup of the fully evolved knowledge-based organization and of the employment picture. Peter Drucker, author of *Managing in A Time of Great Change*, is among those who estimate that by the year 2000 only one-eighth to one-sixth of workers will be employed in what is traditionally referred to as blue-collar work.

Manual jobs will continue to decrease in number. A large percentage of workers will be service workers. The educational requirements will not be as high for service workers, and salaries will reflect this.

In the traditional organization, the division that created conflict, misunderstanding, misinformation and therefore underachievement was management vs. nonmanagement. The potential division that can cause dysfunction in the new organization is the knowledge worker versus other workers, primarily service workers.

## Task and Process

Balancing attention to task and attention to process makes it possible to thrive in the new economy. "Task" and "process" are terms that have become part of reengineering jargon and have taken on specific meanings within that context. The new organization uses the terms somewhat differently.

As described by Michael Hammer in *Beyond Reengineering*, "task" refers to a unit of work performed by one person. A process is a related group of tasks that together create a product of value to the customer. In the new organization, "task orientation" or "task" means focusing on getting the job done — on the outcomes. Behaviors and actions associated with task include being directive and controlling, and making logic-based decisions.

"Process orientation" or "process" means focusing on *how* the job gets done or *how* outcomes are reached. Behaviors and actions associated with process include being facilitative, asking questions and using intuition.

### The Traditional Organization
*The traditional organization is the hierarchical, top-down, command-and-control organization that served us well enough in the old economy.*

### The New Organization
*The new organization is one that successfully crosses into the new economy and thrives in it.*

The rest of this book is dedicated to identifying the requirements of the new organization.

# TOWARD THE NEW ORGANIZATION

Many companies are struggling through the transition. Even organizations that see themselves as successful, at least based on bottom-line performance, have spent too much energy on the struggle. For others, an all-consuming bottom-line focus and organizational anorexic tendencies have been self-destructive. Organizations are living on whatever energy their downsized and emotionally and physically exhausted employee population can muster. Their energy is not being renewed and will eventually be depleted. This energy depletion is a critical issue. How long can we keep running to catch up, keep up, get ahead and stay ahead?

*Energy* is the first critical ingredient for thriving in the new economy. The second is *wisdom*.

The organizations that will thrive in the new economy will be those that have refocused and restructured as needed, allowing them to be fleet of foot. A successful organization will have a highly efficient operation, but so will its competitors. So how will an organization achieve an edge? By developing wisdom.

In the twenty-first century, fast-paced change will continue to be the norm. Successful organizations will be able to respond instantly and intuitively to new and constant information, requiring enormous energy and wisdom. To reach this point of evolution, organizations must achieve substantive change. Even though indicators suggest that the vast majority of organizations are making sincere, and often costly, efforts to bring that change about, too small a percentage are actually achieving it. It has been suggested that only 18 to 20 percent of organizations are achieving substantive change.

## ON BECOMING WISE

Wisdom is perhaps most evidently required in strategic decision-making processes. The best-run company can't succeed if it takes off in the wrong direction, or in the right direction at the wrong time.

In chaotic times, making the right call becomes more complicated. Decision makers must be constantly scanning the environment and be able to instinctively recognize movement and changes in patterns, however small, that may ultimately be significant.

Edward Lorenz's popularized butterfly effect illustrates the magnitude of the challenge. It suggests that the flutter of a butterfly's wings in China can result in significant turbulence in North America two weeks later. A significant message delivered here is one of interconnectedness. Everyone and everything is part of a system. When living in a high-speed system, the need for wisdom becomes accentuated. When we see a flutter of a butterfly's wings out of the corner of our eye, we must quickly decide whether or not it is significant.

There are countless examples in the business world of too little significance being attached to what would later become very significant occurrences. The very best strategic decisions, however, are still not enough. Everyone in the organization must have the wisdom to make the best day-to-day decisions, from capital investment to handling an irate customer, and possess the authority to use that wisdom. This is more acutely important as organizations put a greater emphasis on self-direction, and as the number of people making important decisions increases.

Wisdom requires organizational street-smarts. The successful company instinctively knows how to respond. It has a keen understanding of its industry, environment, stakeholders, customers, competitors and, what is most important, the idiosyncrasies of the new economy.

## GETTING IN FLOW WITH
## THE NEW ECONOMY

Energy and wisdom emerge when we stop struggling and get in flow with the new economy. The first step to getting in flow is understanding the new economy and how the organizations that support it and thrive in it must differ from those of the industrial-based economy.

Becoming settled in the new economy does not mean there will be less change, but it does mean that we will have become more at ease with change. We will have learned to quit struggling and to find order within chaos.

That the transition from the old world economy to the new is a major one filled with economic, social, political and organizational upheaval surprises no one who has been experiencing it. However, as indicated earlier, when we see things close up, we often do not fully recognize their magnitude.

Some suggest that the current transition is the most traumatic period of change in human history. According to Alvin and Heidi Toffler in *Creating a New Civilization*, "It [humanity] faces the deepest social upheaval and creative restructuring of all time. Without clearly recognizing it, we are engaged in building a remarkable new civilization from the ground up." And here we are, blessed or otherwise, depending on our propensity for change, to be living in this dramatic period of history. Each individual and organization has the incredible opportunity to help shape the new, emerging world. Some people and organizations have made the choice to be observers — to wait it out or let it pass. They do not yet realize that "This too shall pass away" does not apply to the change of the new economy. Others have put all of their energy into fighting the challenges, heads down, so focused on the fight they often fail to notice the opportunities whizzing by. We used to say that we have to be ready when opportunity knocks — it doesn't pause long enough to knock any more, but passes by at enormous speeds and we must have our heads up, the wisdom to recognize it and the quick reflexes to grab it.

Most of the differences between the old and new economies are intellectually obvious to anyone who has had at least one eye open in today's world of work. Translating that intellectual knowledge into intrinsic understanding and the resulting consistently appropriate behavior is not as common.

Figure 1

## THE TRANSITION

| INDUSTRIAL-BASED ECONOMY | THE NEW ECONOMY |
|---|---|
| The Traditional Organization Characteristics | The New Organization Characteristics |
| • Slow-paced change | • Fast-paced change |
| • Vertical | • Horizontal |
| • Inward looking | • Outward looking |
| • Focused on task | • Balances focus on task and process |
| • People and work are isolated in compartments | • People and work are interconnected or part of a system |
| • Temporal | • Spiritual |

# GETTING FROM THEN TO NOW — THE CHALLENGES

The transition from the industrial-based economy to the information-based economy is a continuum. Organizations are at different places on the continuum. In fact, different parts within organizations are at different places. This is one of the dilemmas in making it across the transition and settling into the new economy. Some organizations have a foot in each world. They may have moved toward the new economy in structuring a team-based organization, but they also have managers who have not yet made the transition to leadership. They may have removed layers and declared empowerment, but their systems may prevent the ideal from being realized.

When one sector of IBM first developed self-directed teams, the members' ability to actually make decisions and therefore succeed in a self-directed mode was inhibited by their information system. To access information required to make some of their important decisions, they had to enter a management access code into their system. Since no members were managers, no one had such a code. New concepts had been embraced, but the system had not yet caught up to the new way of doing things.

Neither had some of the people in other parts of the large organization. When they called and asked to speak to the manager, they could not accept the response, "We have no manager. I can help you." The team finally came up with a solution. Since they were all self-managed and were carrying management responsibilities, when anyone insisted on speaking to "the manager," the member would respond, "I am a manager. Can I help you?"

The other dilemma is one of grasping how far we must go and to what extent our thinking and behaviors must change in order for us to function in the new world. Alvin Toffler's book *The Adaptive Corporation* impressed me in the early 1980s when I was first exploring how we could better manage the change we were experiencing and the more traumatic change to come. In his book, Toffler talks about his attempt in the early seventies to convince AT&T that it should be broken up. A few people in the organization recognized the validity of what he was saying, but it was too radical a concept for most. His paper went underground where it moved impotently through the company.

Eventually, of course, the breakup of AT&T was forced and the stress and negative spin-offs were much greater than they would have been had the decision come earlier and proactively from within. The message that was printed in my memory was that in order to make it in the new world, we have to be able to think the unthinkable. Decades later companies are still having difficulty heeding Toffler's message.

Because change experienced in many companies has been so traumatic, people assume that they have been thinking the unthinkable and therefore have no further to go. However, these unthinkables such as downsizing, or the creation of virtual hospitals, are products of necessity. Proactively and creatively thinking the unthinkable requires wisdom. Structuring and working in creative ways that are unthinkable today will be the hallmark of the successful organization tomorrow.

It is human nature to want to believe that we have arrived. We have done what needs to be done, the worst is over, now we can get back to some semblance of normality.

In workshops, people often look at the characteristics that are required in an organization in the new economy described in The Transition (Figure 1) and declare, "We're doing all of that." Because their company is doing some things that reflect new-economy behaviors, they believe they have arrived. They rightly feel good about the fact that they perhaps are structured in teams, are paying more attention to the input the world around them offers, or are asking customers what they need rather than prescribing for them.

North American companies made some major strides toward the new organization in the late eighties and early nineties, and deserve to celebrate their success. On the other hand, we must recognize that in the new economy we never arrive. The organization will constantly evolve. This is not a concept with which many logical thinkers and task-oriented individuals, who need a sense of closure to mark their progress, feel comfortable. And we must continue to challenge ourselves with the question, "Are we really thinking the unthinkable?" So let's take a deep breath, pat ourselves on the back for what we have accomplished in the face of incredible challenges, and reflect on how we can struggle less and achieve more. We can thrive in the new economy and do so with ease. Organizations that will be successful will be those that have learned how to do it with ease.

Most companies are on the path to the new organization. Most, too, have some residual characteristics from the old world. We become in sync with the new economy when our organizational behaviors (not just structures or programs) are consistently reflective of the ways of the new world.

## The Pace of Change

The accelerated rate of change is one aspect of the new economy that demands that organizations approach the world very differently. Everyone knows that the only constant today is change. Questions to ask yourself as you look around your organization are: Are *we* really changing? People around me are doing different things, but are they doing things differently? Are most of us simply accepting change, and doing our best to cope, or are we making adjustments to allow us — and the company — to respond more effectively, and experience greater success? Is change in our organization cosmetic or substantive?

Most organizations, for example, put a value on teamwork and have labeled most groups as teams. People may be attending more meetings, participating in task forces and becoming involved in issues that were previously management's, and are carrying a heavier load with more responsibilities. Too frequently, however, behaviors are not modified. Individuals may not think of sharing information; perhaps only a few people actively participate in the team; the leader may still dominate; lack of trust may prevent open communication; solutions may be typical of those who are still thinking vertically and hanging on to preconceived ideas. Therefore, the enhancements experienced by individual team members, the team and the company are minimal, if any.

Consider Total Quality Management (TQM) programs. Huge budgets have been dedicated to these programs. It is not unusual for people to focus on quality in their "quality meetings" where they apply TQM to organizational processes and then leave the concepts behind in the meeting room when they return to their work stations and their day-to-day tasks.

What about ownership of communication processes? There is an increased belief in, and attempt to achieve, consensus. However, in most meetings that I have observed, I see discussion taking place with very little dialogue. True consensus (i.e., willingness to support a decision) is impossible without dialogue. But most people discuss. People are ready to present their own opinions and feel it is their responsibility to persuade others to their point of view. Seldom is there demonstration of the recognition that if dialogue is to take place, each participant must take responsibility for understanding the other person's point of view, rather than putting the onus on the others to "prove it to me."

In these instances, an organization may have put a team structure in place and may advocate consensus, but old behaviors prevent cohesiveness and real consensus. Change initiatives must become part of the organization's fiber to achieve substantive change.

The remaining descriptors of the traditional organization versus the new indicate the behavioral adjustments that will most powerfully connect organizations with the ways of the new economy.

## From Vertical to Horizontal

Anyone who has been in the work force for a few years recognizes the characteristics of the vertical organization: a top-down, command-and-control organization that asks people to bring their bodies to work and just enough of their minds to get the job done and leave the rest — including opinions, creativity and values — at the door. This is probably where the greatest change has been experienced. Long before the flattening of the organization made increased empowerment and self-direction a necessity, there was definite movement toward participatory management and teamwork. Procter and Gamble was experiencing degrees of success in the seventies, and Jack Welch brought participation to GE in the early eighties. Many organizations picked up on the trend, but it was common to hear the expression "They're [management] not walking the talk." Necessity has brought many more to a real belief in shared leadership.

Everyone is not yet living the belief, but this is normal during the transition. People are at different places. Eventually our behaviors will be in sync, either because some people who have taken longer to change will have caught up, have fallen by the wayside or have retired.

The degree to which an organization is functioning horizontally is evident in its communication patterns. In a vertical organization, communication is downward; in healthier vertical organizations, it is also upward. Horizontal communication (between peers and across the company) in a vertical organization is, for the most part, limited to social chit-chat: "How was the weekend?" or "How are the kids?" Work-related conversation is usually limited to the need to have information, which must often be requested because it is seldom volunteered: "Have you got the totals that I need for the report?" or "Has legal approved the changes to XYZ's contract?"

In the horizontal organization, the top-down communication has changed from passing down directions to sharing information. Team members are quickly and fully informed about changes. Bottom-up communication has noticeably increased as management looks to the front line for input and direction. But most remarkable is the quantity and quality of peer-to-peer communication. A much larger portion of discussion is focused on work-related issues. Conversation is not just an exchange of need-to-know information, but an exchange of ideas and a "Hey, it might be useful for you to know . . ." type of dialogue. What is even more important, this information is not just being exchanged in meetings. The richest information and idea exchanges are happening during a walk to the warehouse or over a cup of coffee. The communication is spontaneous and energetic.

In the vertical organization, information is seen as power and is hoarded. In the horizontal organization, there is a recognition that sharing — not hoarding — creates power. Hoarding shuts off connections and actually decreases power; sharing opens connections and increases power. The information also grows more powerful through sharing and building and is turned more readily into the most valuable resource — knowledge (information productively applied).

In the horizontal company, the broadly shared information is not meant to just keep people in the picture. It is meant to be interpreted and used across the organization.

## Inward Looking vs. Outward Looking

In the industrial-based economy, companies were able to get by, even if they had blinders on. Many clopped along using only information they had gained through their own narrow experience and slight view of the world, and they saw only the part of the future that was directly within sight. In that world, problems were tackled by senior people in the company who possessed firsthand experience, unless a consultant was hired. Tackling problems frequently meant laying blame rather than finding solutions. Resources were plentiful, and if something didn't work, the easiest solution was to hire more people or buy more equipment. Staff tried to solve problems by examining what, from their perspective, had worked and what hadn't worked in the past and why or why not. But their view was limited, so newcomers who might have had a fresh perspective were often told that they didn't understand "the way we do things around here."

Inward-looking organizations spend an inordinate amount of time on the little internal stuff. A senior management team, whose meeting I observed as part of teamwork development, spent 30 minutes discussing whether the receptionist should drink coffee at her desk, and 15 minutes on new market strategies.

When Lou Gerstner came into IBM as CEO, one of his first observations was "I've never seen an organization so caught up in its own underwear." Getting caught up in the little internal stuff and "the way we do things" is what drags around the ankles of an inward-looking organization and trips it up. The inward-looking company takes a heads-down approach.

The outward-looking organization has a heads-up, land-ahoy approach. It is constantly scanning the environment. It checks its experience against that of others; it learns from others' successes and failures. It looks for input from customers and acts on it. It knows its industry and its competitors.

We have made terrific headway toward outwardness in the nineties. The area that is the weakest is that of gathering and sifting information, and its application.

Our outward-looking behavior needs to evolve to the point where we are so in tune with our environment that we are automatically and continuously making appropriate adjustments to the changes around us. "Around us" now means globally, not simply our immediate environment. We must look further afield. In addition, the information created is multiplying exponentially. Keeping up to date is becoming an overwhelming task for many. With new technologies, it does not need to be. For the most part, it seems overwhelming because keeping informed is not yet seen as part of the job and is therefore left until last. We deal with it only if the lack of particular information is affecting our ability to do the job (e.g., new product information), or if we will be at a disadvantage with our peers.

Embarrassment used to spur people on to go through the circulated FYI information piling up in their in-basket. They knew they were creating blockage in the information flow pipe and so they would at least briefly glance through the memo or article so they could tick off their names on the circulation sticker and move it along to the next person. Now that more information sharing is happening electronically, that impetus is not there to the same degree.

Workers in the new organization not only keep up to date on information sent to them, but proactively search out new information. Keeping current is part of the job. Technology can give us access to the information we need, but first we must know what information to look for. We must ask the right questions; then comes the collection of information, its interpretation, relevance and application.

### Learning from the Very Old and the Very New

"We are different. That doesn't apply to us." The high and solid walls of the traditional organization create an insular and often elitist mentality that becomes a learning disability for many. Successful organizations have become more outward looking and recognize that not only can they learn from other organizations but they must look beyond the organizational world for lessons. The Saturday morning meeting at the Wal-Mart head office became part of the culture and an event looked forward to, in spite of the fact it was held on a day off. What made it interesting and valuable? Its unpredictable and stimulating agenda. Management thinking was constantly pricked by something as simple as articles people brought in to share with the others, or, at the other extreme, an appearance of a high-profile mystery guest from an industry very different from their own.

From the beginning, Wal-Mart, even before the phrase was coined, was a learning organization. Sam Walton knew the importance of looking outward and continually learning.

Models that support and enrich the new organization are often most clearly demonstrated outside of the traditional world. In the following chapters you will find references to and models from quantum physics, Taoism and Native peoples' culture that offer insights into the new organization.

## Creating Balance

As the world has become more complex, people have searched for complex answers. They look for a eureka experience or, at the very least, something that will take a two-day workshop or a thick book to explain. New and apparently sophisticated solutions such as reengineering have failed to provide The Answer. In the case of reengineering, estimates of its success rate range from 20 percent to 40 percent. Success is bottom-line evidence that things are better, but whether there will be long-term positive results remains to be seen. In other words, the short-term bottom line as a barometer of the health of the organization is an open question.

In the organizational world, we have recognized that too much control, hoarding of power and limited communication result in rigid organizations. The old world was imbalanced. It was highly task oriented and undervalued the process-oriented behaviors and activities that would have provided balance. Being in sync with the new economy requires achieving a fine balance between attention to task and attention to process.

When organizations experience imbalance, they require extra energy to function and energy is misused and wasted. They become dissipative structures. When organizations achieve a finer balance between task and process, they generate the energy required to keep the body running at peak performance and are able to respond with insightful decisions (wisdom) that will direct the body to ongoing success.

Task focus is a vertical approach and focusing on process is a horizontal approach. For example, vertical task-oriented behaviors and activities include directing, prescribing, telling, structuring, logic-based decision making, controlling, paying attention to detail, moving things along and bringing closure. In the industrial-based economy, highly structured, task-focused organizations were the norm.

Horizontal process-oriented behaviors include being facilitative, asking, using intuition, visioning, connecting with others, focusing on the big picture, gathering new information, solving problems creatively, being in tune with people issues and being open to all perspectives. A vertical focus is a heads-down, results-oriented approach. A horizontal focus is a heads-up approach that emphasizes interaction. Vertical focus is inward looking; horizontal focus is outward looking.

The vertical, rigid, lumbering structures of the industrial-based economy are the antithesis of the highly responsive organization that is required in an environment of fast-paced change. Most organizations have changed gears and set about creating responsive organizations. To do that they had to put a greater focus on the horizontal process — or *how* they were getting the job done — which meant increasing participation through more meetings, task forces, cross-functional teams, self-directed teams and a multitude of other initiatives to change the shape and culture of the organization. They became convinced that creating flatter organizations, having team leaders instead of managers, and having employees who were team members or associates, and who were customer focused, vision focused, empowered and therefore motivated, would result in a flexible, responsive and highly successful organization.

In their zeal to remake themselves, many organizations moved too far from vertical structure and task and became too focused on horizontal process. At the inquiry into the fatal subway crash in Toronto in 1995, David Gunn, head of the Toronto Transit Commission, described the organization when he took over. Everyone was spending all of their time in meetings with consultants, he said. Not only were the buses dirty, but they were not being properly maintained. This situation was compounded by serious fiscal restraints. The managers had been "burning the furniture" to keep running.

This did not sound like a description of an organization that had a reputation for excellence and had received accolades for being the safest public transportation system in the world. It was a graphic description of an organization that had achieved excellence in the old world, and was trying to maintain itself through the transition to the new economy. Balancing task and process becomes doubly difficult when at the same time you are juggling financial cutbacks.

When the pendulum swings too far from task to process, there can be too much consultation, too much wheel spinning or reinventing of the wheel, lots of activity and too little action. If attention to horizontal activities is not effectively balanced with attention to vertical, task-oriented activities, frustration results and the culture seldom changes. Behind the meetings and the activities, behavior often reverts to a control mentality to try to compensate for something that appears to be (and perhaps is) out of control. The complete transformation of a culture takes time, plus highly effective, well-structured processes.

The TTC example is blatant. Other examples are more subtle. A vertical/horizontal balance does not only refer to getting the organization's key task completed while still meeting, communicating and sharing decisions; it means that there is an appropriate amount of horizontal process in every task and an appropriate amount of vertical structure in every process.

Balance does not mean equal vertical orientation and horizontal orientation. It means the appropriate degree of each. Most frequently it means a much greater focus on process activities than in the past with enough vertical structure to ensure productive outcomes. Gone are the comfortable days when we could turn to the experts for solutions or methodically develop a reassuring five-year plan, and with some good management even see it implemented. New unexplored territory has no experts and relies on risk-taking, innovative pioneers to provide the breakthrough solutions. Plans are never complete but always evolving as circumstances change. Decision makers working in ambivalent situations cannot rely on logic alone. They need to tap others' insights, to think creatively and intuitively, and to be well informed so that everyone has an understanding of all the variables and ramifications. These aspects of the new world can leave highly task-oriented individuals uncomfortably wriggling in their seats, wiping sweaty hands on their pant legs.

It is relatively easy to recognize a gross imbalance. It is not as easy to achieve the very fine balance that produces the wisdom and energy that equal success in the new world.

Creating balance means learning which aspects of process need to be added and how to develop the required skills discussed later, such as intuitive thinking, dialoguing and information scanning. It also means learning how to add the right amount of task and structure, where it is needed and how it can most effectively be added.

## Working in Compartments vs. Working in a System

Understanding the new economy and the type of organization that will thrive within it requires an intrinsic understanding of systems thinking and our interconnectedness. Systems thinking, most simply put, is the understanding that everything we do affects everyone else and what everyone else does affects us. We are all part of everything and contribute to, or diminish, everything. How different from the "That's not my job," "That's their problem," or "That's none of their business" attitudes of the traditional, rigid, compartmentalized organization where turfdoms abounded.

We now realize there is no *we* and *they* — there is only *we*. The horizontal organization as well as the heightened need for interconnectedness reinforce the model of the team-based organization. Interconnectedness requires that individuals see the link between themselves and others inside and outside of teams, that teams see the connection with other teams, and that the organization and its parts see the myriad of external connections with partners, suppliers, customers and competitors — and respond accordingly. These are not only visible connections such as meetings, data collected, communication or information shared. Everyone must be aware of the invisible connections as well; for example, how what one team does will affect another or how a competitor's new product will impact on them.

Many new and unlikely partnerships are being forged in the new world and teams within the organization are quickly changing. Interconnectedness requires new skills and a new mindset for many, plus a belief in their importance. Without that belief, people will forget, put their heads back down and miss important connections.

# THE VALUE-BASED ORGANIZATION — WHERE NICE GUYS FINISH FIRST

Barriers and walls have been torn down. The organization is becoming permeable. We are beginning to recognize that we are part of a system.

What used to fit inside neat boxes no longer does. Values and beliefs that used to be left at the door of the organization at first hovered at the doorstep and now have entered and are becoming integrated into the organization.

The inside and the outside of the traditional organization are two completely different worlds. There is business dress for work and casual dress outside of work. Certain language at work, other language outside work. Words like love, caring and spirituality create discomfort at the work place. Inside, friendship is cautious. Can people be friends and still work together effectively? Children are part of the outside life and never intrude on our inside life.

When people arrive at work in the traditional organization, they leave most of themselves at the door: their opinions, critical abilities, values, personal beliefs, many of their talents, often their joy — in essence, themselves. The body comes to work, but the whole person stays outside, waiting to be picked up on the way out.

In some of my workshops, I use a questionnaire that addresses personal styles. Frequently I am asked, "Should I answer this the way I am at work or the way I am the rest of the time?" Little wonder the level of stress in the workplace is so high! Not only is the load incredibly heavy for most people, but they are taking on what they believe to be the expected persona.

In some organizations, a new wholeness is beginning to appear as inside and outside are beginning to merge. Most organizations have some form of casual Fridays and, in general, business dress is becoming more casual; daycare centers are appearing onsite and some working environments even allow parents to take children to work; fitness facilities are common; values and feelings are more readily discussed; laughter and chatter, once a cause for concern, are now a sign of health; the workplace has begun to become humanized, and by the year 2000, 40 percent of people will be working at home.

Many factors have come together to spark the healthier, more humanistic and value-based organization. The visioning and values exercises of the eighties began the process of bringing beliefs into the workplace and recognizing their ability to enhance outcomes. People began exploring New Age thinking and the spiritual side of themselves. The percentage of people interested in the spiritual is not known, but judging by the number of bestsellers on these subjects, the numbers are huge. When people go to work, how long can they be expected to leave their fundamental beliefs at the door?

The stresses of a complex and changing world create a need for something that can be counted on, some basic truths and principles that will sustain people and energize them, even though the world around them is chaotic. The emergence of the value-based or spiritual organization is inevitable. Some organizations will ignore or even try to suppress it. Others will make some attempt to emulate it because it will become politically correct. Leading organizations will be espousing it, but they may not be completely comfortable with its requirements.

A value-based organization *lives* by certain principles — not just values that enhance the company's external image such as quality and customer service, but principles that it lives and breathes by, makes decisions by and treats employees by.

The new organization is forced to examine not only what it does but what it intends to do. A corporation may look like a great corporate citizen when it donates funds to build a new opera house. But is it really a philanthropic gesture or a marketing opportunity?

Advocates of the value-based organization are not suggesting that tax credits be scratched or that promotional opportunities be ignored, but ask: Would the corporation be willing to fill a need that did not offer these in return? Does it make grand gestures only, or does it live by its principles moment to moment? How does it support the individual worker with daycare problems?

The value-based organization looks at ethical issues that most corporations avoid, such as greed: what is it, and can an organization ever make too much profit?

Most important, the value-based organization ensures that everyone — employees, suppliers, customers — is treated with care. Not only does the organization treat employees with understanding and respect, but employees treat one another with the same appreciation.

The trust and caring that develop in a spiritual organization enrich the connections resulting in powerful interconnectedness. As connections open and stress is alleviated, energy blockers are removed. The organization revitalizes.

The value-based organization is the ultimate recognition of a systems organization. Everyone and every action affects everyone else and everything else for better or for worse. Living by this recognition creates a powerful organization.

The philosophy of the value-based organization in a nutshell is "Do unto others. . . ." The simplicity of the concept is deceiving. Treating others as you would be treated is easy to accept as a reasonable idea. Living up to it is another thing, as most individuals discover. How much more difficult for complex organizations to be spiritually focused.

W. Edwards Demming, the American credited with creating Japanese Management, many years ago pinpointed the management's weak spot that so often derailed well-intentioned quality initiatives. Management, he observed, lacked "the constancy of purpose." Constancy of purpose requires belief. But perhaps more important, it requires a system that ensures consistent demonstration of the belief. We are back to balance — belief on the process side must be balanced by plan and structure on the task side. We examine the architecture of the value-based organization in chapters 14 and 15.

The first part of each chapter presents concept and theory along with some illustrative examples. Should you be looking for an overview of *Organization 2000*, those pages probably provide you with enough detail.

Should you be looking for strategies to strengthen your ability and that of your organization to thrive in the new economy, you will likely be interested in Theory in Action and Reflection & Application. Theory in Action, found in the latter part of most chapters, provides more specific case examples of how both private- and public-sector organizations have successfully applied some of the theory and concepts applied in the chapter. Reflection & Application, which appears at the end of many chapters, provides questions to challenge your thinking about the concepts presented, and tools and instruments to support you in applying the ideas in your organization.

---

# REFLECTION & APPLICATION

## Making the Transition

How far is your organization in its move from the traditional organization to the new organization?

Figure 2

## THE TRANSITION EVALUATION

Identify the degree to which your organization has moved from a traditional organization to a new organization by rating each pair of characteristics on a scale of 1 to 4.

| INDUSTRIAL-BASED ECONOMY | | | | THE NEW ECONOMY |
|---|---|---|---|---|
| The Traditional Organization Characteristics | | | | The New Organization Characteristics |
| ▪ Slow-paced change | 1 2 3 4 | | | ▪ Fast-paced change |
| ▪ Vertical | 1 2 3 4 | | | ▪ Horizontal |
| ▪ Inward looking | 1 2 3 4 | | | ▪ Outward looking |
| ▪ Focused on task | 1 2 3 4 | | | ▪ Balances focus on task and process |
| ▪ People and work are isolated in compartments | 1 2 3 4 | | | ▪ People and work are inter-connected or part of a system |
| ▪ Temporal | 1 2 3 4 | | | ▪ Spiritual |

### Interpretation

**6-12** Your organization functions in a traditional fashion. It may have experienced success in the industrial-based economy but will struggle in the new.

**13-18** Your organization has begun to develop "new world" behaviors. Focus and consistency are required to ensure it continues to move forward.

**19-23** Your organization has the ability to function well in the new economy. Vigilance is required to ensure you have a firm foothold.

**24** Your organization is in sync with the new economy.

1. Consider the characteristics of the new organization as they were described in this chapter. Use the evaluation form above to

measure your organization's progress in developing each of the required characteristics.

2. Reflect on the following: Thriving in the new economy requires the organization to balance its attention to task and its attention to process in all of its activities.

*Decision making:*

• Is there a balance between task and process in the way your company makes decisions? For example, when breakthrough decisions are required, do you involve people who are not experts and so are not bound by the traditional paradigms?

• Do you consciously use methods that awaken right-brain creative thinking?

• When decisions are made, do you effectively balance discussion and participation with coming to closure and producing timely outcomes?

*Working independently:*

• Do you balance your attention to task and attention to process when you work independently? For example, do you work efficiently on your own but recognize when to put your head up and get input from others?

• Do you combine logical, step-by-step problem solving with innovation and creativity?

• Do you challenge your own thinking?

• Do you deliberately turn to people who think very differently from the way you do — perhaps with whom you often strongly disagree — for their input and perspective?

• Do you keep others informed about what you are doing?

• Do you share information that might be useful to others?

# Part I

# STILLING THE PENDULUM

The following section describes how organizations and individuals can achieve the fine balance required in their attention to task and attention to process. It describes the basics that must be present and how they can be strengthened in organizations. Peruse this section before reading it in detail. If you believe you and your organization have effectively achieved the balance described, move ahead to the next section, Becoming Wise.

# 1

# THE YIN AND YANG OF THE ORGANIZATION

At the beginning of time there were twin spirits known as Teharonhiawagon, or the Creator, and Tawiskarn, or the Evil Mind. The Evil Mind fashioned much of what was considered bad in the world, including poisonous plants and the hatred that can live in the human heart. Meanwhile, the Creator lovingly made the first people out of lumps of clay. Both of the twins were essential to the creation of the world.

For the Iroquois people, a sense of interdependent and reciprocal polarities is a foundation piece of their culture. It is not a matter of choosing one over the other, but of incorporating both. Together they create the whole.

Balance as a basic life need has been extolled by mystics, sages, psychologists, ecologists and New Age thinkers. Left and right brain, feminine and masculine, Mars and Venus, Yin and Yang have become popular concepts. Each member of each pair has something unique and essential to offer: the members can be in balance and complement one another and so create great harmony and superior outcomes, or they can be out of balance, one member of the pair exerting more influence, resulting in conflict and inferior outcomes.

*Task and process are the Yin and Yang of the organization.* For many years our organizations have been out of balance, favoring task over process. We got away with imbalance when times were good by compensating with hiring more staff or purchasing new equipment to enhance productivity and quality. When the pace of change was slower, we had time to catch up even if we were limping from imbalance. As the pace of change continued to accelerate and companies faced an economic crunch, it became all too clear that the rigid, highly task-oriented, hierarchical organization was an anachronism in the information age. In an attempt to correct what were seen as the task-oriented problems — too much structure and control, and too little communication, participation and ownership on the part of members — organizations swung their attention to process. Some now became as dearly attached to process as they had been to task. In their zeal to remake themselves, they frenetically called meetings, formed committees, talked about values, anointed teams and empowered people. Many became too highly process oriented with insufficient structure and direction from the task side to create a balance. Instead of achieving the needed flexibility and responsiveness, many organizations have become limp. Therefore, they experience ineffective participation, wheel spinning, mediocre decisions, lack of consensus, lack of clarity as to parameters of authority and confusion over who is accountable.

In Chinese culture, the poles of cosmic energy are Yin (negative) and Yang (positive). They are associated with feminine and masculine energies, and represent such qualities as the yielding and the firm, the weak and the strong.

On a personal level, Yang is the personality and Yin is the soul. Soul is the essence or life force. The Yang or personality is what expresses or suppresses it.

The essence or life force of the organization lies within the process. When there is a balance between task and process, priorities and behaviors, the organization's life force is released.

Balance involves the principle of polarity. The principle of balanced and reciprocal polarities underlies the basic beliefs of many cultures. In Western culture and in the traditional organization, we tend to think of polarities as opposing one another. Instead of understanding the balance of polarities, we frequently see the opposites as good or bad and one overcoming the other, such as light and darkness, life and death.

Alan Watts, who was dedicated to interpreting Eastern philosophy to the West, suggested that the Western world has difficulty accepting the concept of balance, because balance doesn't suggest progress or winning, which our linear minds require for a sense of accomplishment. In *Tao: The Watercourse Way*, he writes, "Indeed, the whole enterprise of Western technology is 'to make the world a better place,' to have pleasure without pain, wealth without poverty, and health without sickness. But as is now becoming obvious, our violent efforts to achieve this ideal with weapons such as DDT, penicillin and nuclear energy are creating more problems than they solve. We have been interfering with a complex system of relationships which we don't understand. As we try to comprehend and control the world it runs away with us."

The attempt to control creates greater imbalance and dysfunction. We revert too far toward one pole and then inevitably try to compensate and swing too far back to the other, as is often the case when managers swing back and forth from control to empowerment.

A different, and very ancient, view is that polarities do not oppose one another but are different aspects of the same system. The positive and negative poles of electricity do not compete; one is not better than the other; one will not overpower and eliminate the other. Both are part of the essence of the system.

We are only just beginning to understand the importance of managing polarity in the organization. Barry Johnson, who believes that polarity management is essential to an organization's success, describes polarity this way: "Polarities to manage are sets of opposites which can't function well independently. Because the two sides of the pole are interdependent, you cannot choose one as a 'solution' and neglect the other. The objective of polarity management is to get the best of both opposites while avoiding the limits of each."

When something isn't working, a natural response is to do a complete about face and switch to the opposite pole. Organizations have swung from control to empowerment, from individual work to teamwork. When the swing is drastic, old problems may be resolved, but new difficulties may be created. Sometimes when organizations first empower people, managers believe they cannot intervene, even if things are dangerously careening off the tracks. In other cases, once the team concept has been adopted, everything happens in teams with no consideration as to whether a team approach is most appropriate for a particular issue or task.

In Western culture, instead of balancing polarities there is frequently a sense of good or bad and one overcoming the other such as light and darkness, life and death. From the organizational world we can add control and empowerment.

This kind of imbalance in a system, whether the ecosystem, the human body or an organization, results in dysfunction. Symptoms of dysfunction in the organization may be dramatic, such as negative bottom-line results or loss of market share, or they may be a myriad of aches and pains such as mediocre outcomes, decisions that don't take or reengineering efforts that disappoint.

Imbalances may occur in the strategic decision processes or in any or many of the thousands of processes that together determine the health of the organization — teamwork, meetings or individual front-line decisions and interactions. Organizational balance has always been important, but is more critical in the new economy. The world has found a new balance point. Technology and the breakdown of economic, political and national barriers mean a much more open, horizontal, process-oriented world, whether we are ready for it or not. The rigid, highly structured and compartmentalized traditional organization fit comfortably in the old world. It is discordant with the new and is therefore ineffectual.

In addition, when a system is in a state of imbalance, as a large percentage of organizations are, any spanner thrown into the already teetering works can throw the system into total dysfunction. During the transition to the new economy, problems come from all directions. Once we are settled in the new economy, unpredictable elements will still be present but will not pose as great a threat because the new organization will have achieved sufficient balance and the unexpected will not as easily disrupt the works. Organizational balance is achieved when members are aware of the need for balance, assess the balance in each activity or process and make adjustments as required.

The sooner organizations can find their personal equilibrium, the faster they will settle into the new economy and achieve the exceptional levels of performance required to stay there.

# 2

# THE BALANCING ACT

As in most balancing acts, incorporating the right amount of task and the right amount of process entails the conscious assessment of what is required and then practicing putting all of the elements together. Eventually it becomes instinctive. IBM recognized early the need for an increased focus on horizontal behaviors in order to balance its traditionally vertical behaviors. When I first met people at IBM in the early 1980s, corridor walls were lined with team pictures and personal awards. Most work groups in the area where I was working referred to themselves as teams. Input to important issues was often invited. It appeared that much was being done to increase the company's process orientation.

It is not easy, however, for a company the size of IBM to turn symbols and rhetoric into substance. The pendulum swung widely from one extreme to the other. On the task side, behind the team pictures were familiar laments typical of the old, rigid, hierarchical world. There were concerns about top-down management, lack of communication and a level of competitiveness that made team an incongruent concept. On the process side, at times, there was overparticipation.

A dramatic example is described by Bill Gates. In *The Road Ahead*, he tells of how IBM and Microsoft attempted to form a partnership to develop the OS/2. The partnership was unsuccessful. One of the obstacles faced, in Gates's view, was IBM's belief in full participation. All parts of the organization were kept informed on design plans and invited to give input. The IBM/Microsoft design team received ten thousand recommendations for design change, each of which was discussed.

# VERTICAL AND HORIZONTAL BEHAVIORS

Finding the balance takes specific and consistently demonstrated practices. Enormous upheaval occurred before the efforts initiated by many change agents in various corners of IBM began to result in the truly substantive change that the company began to experience in the early 1990s.

Figure 2.1

## VERTICAL AND HORIZONTAL BEHAVIORS AND ACTIVITIES

| VERTICAL (Task Focused) | HORIZONTAL (Process Focused) |
|---|---|
| ∎Doing | ∎Thinking |
| ∎Working independently | ∎Participating/teamwork |
| ∎Making logic based decisions | ∎Using creativity and intuition |
| ∎Acting | ∎Talking |
| ∎Moving things along | ∎Exploring ideas more deeply |
| ∎Focusing on details | ∎Focusing on the big picture |
| ∎Directing | ∎Facilitating |
| ∎Bringing things to closure (Making decisions) | ∎Opening up/looking for other ideas (Generating alternatives) |
| ∎Controlling | ∎Letting go and empowering |
| ∎Telling | ∎Asking |
| ∎Focusing on the job | ∎Focusing on the people, values, vision |
| ∎Resistant to change | ∎Receptive to change |

Vertical behaviors reflect the traditional organization that worked well in the industrial-based economy. They fit comfortably within a top-down, highly structured mind-set: do as I say, command and control, stay within your own boundaries and don't think too much. Vertical behaviors and activities include setting goals and objectives, moving things along, checking details, directing, making logic-based decisions, bringing things to closure, getting the job done, telling, controlling.

Horizontal behaviors and activities are requisite to the flexible, responsive organization of the new economy. They include visioning, attention to values, focusing on the big picture, creative and intuitive problem solving and decision making, teamwork, participation, communication, gathering new information, brainstorming and tuning in to others' feelings and needs.

Figure 2.2

## BALANCING THE ORGANIZATION

| RIGID | FLEXIBLE (THE NEW ORGANIZATION) | LIMP |
|---|---|---|
| Highly task focused | Balances attention to task and process | Highly process focused |
| Characteristics | Characteristics | Characteristics |
| ▪Decisions made by most powerful members | ▪Shared leadership | ▪Over participation |
| ▪Run by rules and regulations | ▪Self-direction | ▪Too little structure |
| ▪Few meetings, for information only | ▪Open sharing of information | ▪Too frequent meetings |
| ▪Lacks openness and trust | ▪Commitment to common vision | ▪Too few outcomes |
| ▪Resistant to change | | ▪Proliferation of task forces/committees |
| | | ▪Appearance of openness, trust and goodwill |
| Results | Results | Results |
| ▪Slow response | ↑Flexibility and responsiveness | ▪Slow response |
| ▪Ineffective implementation of change | ↑Ownership, commitment | ▪Ineffective implementation of change |
| ▪Low commitment level | ↑Quality, productivity | ▪Low commitment level |
| ▪Inability to achieve beyond minimum performance requirements | ↑Innovation | ▪Inability to achieve beyond minimum performance requirements |

To both vertical- and horizontal-oriented activities and behaviors you can apply the adage that warns about "too much of a good thing." The traditional organization was overdirected, overstructured and overcontrolled. What was missing were the balancing process-oriented behaviors.

There can also be too much emphasis on the process side. Lack of an appropriate degree of vertical focus results in limpness—a lot of activity and perhaps great ideas that go nowhere. Limpness harbors all of the ills of the rigid organization, but adds a sense of frustration and confusion. The new horizontally oriented concepts, systems and behaviors are championed — more meetings, increased participation and group work — and are often erroneously labeled as teamwork. However, the essential vertical or task-oriented components such as structure, direction and focus have been lost. The intent is well meaning but the outcomes rather dismal.

Limp organizations produce several common complaints, such as too many meetings and too few outcomes. Decision making takes too long. People are empowered to make decisions they are not equipped to make. There is too much reinventing of the wheel. Unrealistic expectations are established around teamwork and empowerment leading to disappointment and disillusionment when these new initiatives don't work. Management reverts back to a vertical style when the going gets tough. These organizations do not achieve the substantive change they had hoped for.

The flexible organization effectively integrates the appropriate degree of task and process, given a particular situation. The greater the flexibility (the ability to work comfortably in both task and process modes), the greater the new organization's success.

---

A man walked by a work site and saw three bricklayers. He approached the first and asked, "What are you doing?" The fellow responded, "Making a living." The man went up to the second worker and asked the same question, and the answer he received was, "Laying bricks." He approached the third bricklayer and asked, "What are you doing?" The bricklayer responded, "Me? I'm building a cathedral!"

The story of the bricklayers emphasizes the importance of vision. It is also a vivid example of the importance of balancing vertical and horizontal perspectives. I recently asked participants in a workshop to discuss what they saw as the differences between the fellow who responded "Laying bricks"—the heads-down, task-oriented individual—and the one who responded "Building a cathedral"—the worker whose response suggested an outward-looking process orientation. One participant said, "The guy who said he was laying the bricks is probably doing all of the work." His response triggered a great deal of laughter from others who could identify with his comment. They had experienced highly process-oriented people who were great at visioning and "blue skying" but weren't so great at following through and getting the job done.

The ideal situation, of course, is when the fellow who sees himself building a cathedral is also a dedicated and hard-working bricklayer. But the balancing act goes far beyond that. Looking outward and having the big picture of the cathedral in mind, or even talking about it, is of little use if it is not used productively.

Knowing he is building a cathedral gives the bricklayer information he can use. He might pick up a brick with a flaw in it and toss it aside; it perhaps is good enough for a more modest building, but it is not good enough for a cathedral. Having the big picture of the cathedral in mind, he also realizes when it is important to connect with the other workers.

The process of visioning when aligned with the task results in concrete action that enhances the outcome. Horizontal activities such as visioning, generating ideas or participating are not meant to be ends in themselves, but are designed to enhance getting the job done. One might ask, "Isn't that just common sense?" Yes, but its lack of application is a frequent cause of imbalance.

An extreme example of a horizontal process being seen as an end in itself took place in a health-care organization. I met some of its members at a time when it was having a great deal of difficulty getting people to participate. Some members of the organization cited the following incident that had taken place earlier as the cause of people's reluctance to participate.

The CEO, recognizing the need for a mission statement, had organized an off-site retreat. Members from across the organization were invited to participate in the development of the statement. The CEO facilitated the process. By the end of the day, the group had developed their mission statement and were enthusiastic and proud to have been part of the process. The CEO congratulated them on what they had accomplished and then flipped open his briefcase and handed out pre-printed copies of the statement they thought they had just developed. The CEO had previously written the mission statement and had led them to the same point.

People in the organization, not surprisingly, felt that the process had been dishonest and that the CEO had been manipulative. This wasn't actually the case. If he had been manipulative, he would have been more subtle. Nevertheless, here was someone who misunderstood the entire participation process. He believed the participation process to be the motivator, not realizing that the real motivator is not the process but the outcome, the sense of accomplishment that results from a productive process that produces unique outcomes owned by the group.

The key, then, is not just putting the pieces in place that suggest a horizontally oriented, outward-looking organization. It is not that difficult to put the pieces in place. Costly, perhaps, but not particularly difficult. Most companies have vision, mission and values statements, have established teams, have changed managers' and supervisors' titles to "team leader" and have introduced quality management programs. Too few have managed to create the balance that these initiatives should achieve. Some are making a concerted and impressive effort to do so.

---

## THEORY IN ACTION

Sun Life recognized the need to move from a traditional top-down organization to a more interactive, empowering, process-oriented company if it were to continue to succeed in the new world of heightened competition, deregulation of the financial industry and general unpredictability. In 1991, it selected particular sites to establish Prism Teams. These were work units charged with the challenge of improving their areas of responsibility.

One site that has experienced particular success is the Canadian Central Information Services Group. Outcomes include decreasing their "number one" problems (those which have had the greatest impact on customer service and the bottom line) by 75 percent over three years. Here is substantive — not cosmetic — change.

In their initial planning processes, the Central Information Services

Group had a great enthusiasm for and commitment to the team concept. They also intuitively knew that structure and focus had to balance the interactive processes. Their vice-president, Ross Berrouard, championed the new concept. He was not only involved at the kickoff but stayed actively involved throughout the first year. His presence demonstrated to the new teams that there was serious company commitment to the new way of working. It also ensured a strategic focus. The planning group did not hand the whole process over to unprepared teams and give them a broad directive to work together to make improvements, as many less successful organizations have. Instead, they ensured that teams received skills-development opportunities. They put parameters in place, and specific targets were attached to a reward program. These parameters and targets encouraged increased collaboration to identify and implement ideas that focused on the same strategic priorities, including resolving serious problems, enhancing customer service and decreasing outages. This ensured that energy was directed and ideas aligned, and greatly increased the cumulative power and outcomes of the teamwork.

On the vertical, task side, the group established strategic goals. The targets, expectations and parameters were clear. Outcomes were measured. On the horizontal, process side, teamwork, collaboration, communication and innovation were emphasized.

The impressive outcomes are a result of an ongoing effort to ensure balance. As the team concept matures, this Sun Life group is continuing to increase its horizontal focus. For example, it wants to ensure that thinking does not get trapped within the work units but that all teams are outward looking, both aware of, and taking responsibility for, the greater team. To this end a new parameter was added: 20 percent of ideas implemented were to be neighborhood ideas (generated by cross-functional endeavors).

Companies that achieve substantive change value the management of the process just as they value the management of the task. They establish both task and process-focused goals, which are clearly communicated to the work units and teams throughout the organization. The teams in turn identify areas in which they must achieve in order to meet the expectations of the organization and develop their own task and process-focused goals accordingly. The team's progress is measured regularly against the goals.

Figure 2.3

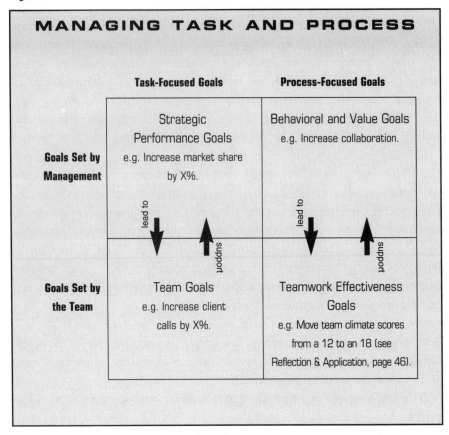

It is common practice to put goals in place on the task side. It is less common to set targets to help manage the process side. In 1993, Unum established a People Goal, which measures success on several value-based dimensions, including pride of an owner, mind of a customer, value differences, acceptance and recognition, sharing and discovering better ways. A five-year improvement target was established. Every year employees respond to a series of questions. The results indicate the degree to which each dimension is being demonstrated in each of Unum's companies. Both improvements and backslides are published across Unum. Successes are celebrated and compensation rewards are provided.

Documented backslides, or slower-than-expected improvement, provide important early information about areas that require attention. Unum's

People Goal offers a means of managing the process side of the organization. The task/process balance within each activity needs to be monitored until it becomes automatic. Imbalance is more evident and more detrimental in some activities than others—teamwork and meetings, for example.

Figure 2.4

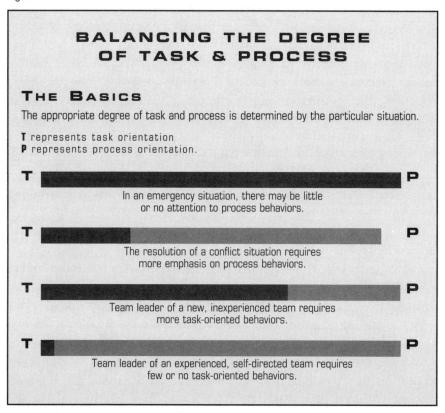

## BALANCING TEAMS

It is often assumed that if a group is labeled a team and is working together, that this is indicative of a process orientation. However, most teams spend little time on process. They put their heads down and focus on task. Effective teams put as much effort into managing the process as they do managing the task. In fact, many teams do not even manage the task.

## Attention to Task

One advantage a sports team has over most work teams is the clarity of its task. Win the game. Do whatever is necessary to score. The clarity and immediacy of the goals allow sports teams to constantly measure performance and ultimately celebrate success. They know when they are slipping, can regroup and reassess their strategy.

Most work teams benefit from developing and using team goals, which are often customer-focused — goals that measure the effectiveness with which customer needs (either internal or external) are being met. These goals allow work teams to assess regularly specific aspects of their performance, celebrate when they score and regroup as needed. These are goals set not by the organization but by the team. They highlight the areas in which the team members must succeed if they are to meet the targets or performance objectives set for them by the organization. For example, a sales and service team identified on-time delivery, decreased response time to customer inquiries and fewer incidents of customers left on hold on the telephone as their customer-focused goals. They found that their customer retention and satisfaction rates quickly improved.

There are many additional benefits of developing customer-focused goals. The process of developing and committing to the goals increases the team's cohesiveness, and gives members the opportunity to explore and to come to agreement on priorities. Lack of agreement on priorities is a frequent source of conflict. It may be sparked by something as simple as one person believing that a customer request should be responded to in two hours, while someone else thinks two days is reasonable.

Teams that set customer-focused goals show rapid performance improvement. Having team members set the goals ensures that the areas that most require improvement are addressed (they are the experts) and helps to ensure their commitment to the performance improvement effort.

## Attention to Process

Managing the process requires regular examination of the process: How effectively are we working together? It is easy to forget process. "We don't have time!" is the usual excuse. However, not managing the process guarantees that the team will not work to its full potential.

Most teams require some type of system to remind the group to manage the process. The team might decide to meet every week to discuss the team process. Members might check the team's health by completing a team-effectiveness assessment regularly, every two to four months. (See Meeting and Team Climate Assessments in Reflection & Application at the end of the chapter.)

If consistent practices are not in place, process is quickly forgotten and the team slips back into a task-only mode. Once the team forgets to manage process, it becomes imbalanced.

As processes, teams and organizations mature, the degree of task versus process required for balance changes. People become more comfortable in a horizontally focused workplace. They learn how to demonstrate horizontal behavior and how to manage horizontal activities. At this more developed stage, balance requires that horizontal activities and behaviors receive greater emphasis, and vertical activities and behaviors are lessened. However, in early stages of development, it is critical that initiatives be supported by sufficient structure (a task dimension).

The CEO of a manufacturing firm believed strongly in teamwork. Before he had arrived, the company had had a highly traditional and autocratic environment. He saw enormous people-potential that was not being tapped. With a great deal of enthusiasm and commitment, he initiated self-directed teams. Almost overnight, the role of supervisor disappeared; some supervisors became team leaders and several front-line people were also selected as team leaders. The challenges were great. Suddenly people who had been used to looking to someone else for the answers had to look to themselves. People who had never had the opportunity of leading were trying to fulfill that challenging role. As participation became the rule, people were expected to attend more meetings. In spite of the challenges, people were enthusiastic. The CEO modeled the team concept and inspired the new team leaders. Everyone was committed to making it work. And it did. Impressive achievements were made in safety, production and quality. In general, morale across the organization was high and people commented that communication between departments had never been better. Success was achieved by sheer enthusiasm.

Gradually, some cracks began to show. Attendance at meetings dropped. Management had concerns that, in spite of training, team leaders did not show enough initiative, did not take responsibility for communication and did not manage performance as effectively as they could. Team leaders were frustrated that expectations were sometimes not clear. They were overloaded, trying to fulfill a leadership role, carry their line job and attend meetings. Production and quality began to slip and conflict became evident among departments.

In spite of a company's enthusiasm and genuine commitment demonstrated by initiatives such as a comprehensive leadership-development program, a powerful vision could be short-lived because of too little vertical focus.

Here was a group of leaders, most of whom were task-oriented individuals, who had worked in a very structured vertical environment performing a line job with clear-cut expectations. Suddenly they were in a horizontal environment in roles that were evolving for them and the organization. In order to function well, they required structured support. While expecting the leaders to immediately take ownership and responsibility, managers did not realize that they were not providing sufficient structure to support the leaders in taking on new responsibilities.

Key elements were missing: clear definitions across the organization of what was meant by "team leader" and how that differed from "supervisor"; specific performance expectations of team leaders; clear parameters of authority; and more highly structured communication and meetings. A more vertical focus was required if the new team-based organization was to achieve long-term success.

### Balancing Meetings

A few years ago, charting vertical and horizontal behaviors in a meeting would produce an overload of vertical behavior — lots of telling and little dialogue. More often today, meeting behaviors are much more process oriented, but too frequently at the expense of outcomes.

A marketing team found that its meetings were frustratingly ineffective. The members engaged in a lot of wheel spinning, or a decision was reached often without the full support of the group. In an attempt to strengthen their meeting effectiveness, the team assessed its task/process balance by reviewing task and process meeting behaviors in the context of one particular meeting. They identified those behaviors that had been most strongly demonstrated and those that had been most conspicuously absent, and these were noted on the Task/Process Meeting Assessment (see Figure 2.5). The team came to recognize that the task and process behaviors identified as being missing were consistently missing in their meetings and were the cause of their ineffectiveness. Commitment to temper the too strong behaviors and to better demonstrate those that had been missing brought quick and significant performance improvement.

Developing vertical task goals comes naturally to most groups. Developing horizontal process goals does not. If, however, the group or organization does not have process goals that are regularly measured and reviewed, productive processes usually fall by the wayside. Eventually, as balance becomes a habit, it will not be necessary to establish separate task and process goals. Goals, activities and behaviors will automatically integrate both. Some organizations believe this is happening for them now. However, I find that seldom is the balance fine tuned. Most organizations are just limping along.

Figure 2.5

## TASK/PROCESS MEETING ASSESSMENT

|  | Task-Oriented Meeting Behaviors and/or Activities | Process-Oriented Meeting Behaviors and/or Activities |
|---|---|---|
| **Present** <br> *Behaviors demonstrated in the meeting* | Covering all items <br> Coming to closure <br> Focusing on details <br> Presenting information <br> Thinking vertically | Ensuring full participation <br> Focusing on the big picture |
| **Missing** <br> *Behaviors that were absent but would have increased the meeting's effectiveness had they been present* | Clarifying objectives <br> Staying on track <br> Identifying action items | Ensuring open communication <br> Exploring individual differences <br> Using a consensus process <br> Thinking creatively |

# REFLECTION & APPLICATION

You might use the following to assess your meeting and team effectiveness.

## 1. Balancing the Meeting

Respond to the following:

1. We leave our meetings with a sense of accomplishment.
   - ❏ Never
   - ❏ Sometimes
   - ❏ Often
   - ❏ Always
2. Our meetings produce quality outcomes.
   - ❏ Never
   - ❏ Sometimes
   - ❏ Often
   - ❏ Always
3. Members are supportive of the outcomes.
   - ❏ Never
   - ❏ Sometimes
   - ❏ Often
   - ❏ Always

This is the intuitive test for task/process balance: If we leave meetings feeling that what we have accomplished is commendable in quantity and quality, and that all participants support the outcomes, there is a strong likelihood that the group is working in balance.

The danger in this method of testing balance is in the evaluation of quality. For example, could the quality have been better if we had more effectively tapped the ideas of the quieter members? Does anyone play devil's advocate or do we come to agreement too quickly?

## 2. Assessing Task/Process Balance in Meetings

Refer to the list of task/process meeting activities and behaviors (Figure 2.6), and assess a recent meeting by completing the meeting assessment (Figure 2.7) on page 46.

Figure 2.6

# MEETING BEHAVIORS

**VERTICAL TASK-FOCUSED MEETING BEHAVIORS**

- Clarify objectives
- Stay on track and on time
- Come to closure/make decisions
- Present information
- Tell/present own perspective
- Focus on details
- Use vertical thinking (logic)
- Focus on the issue
- Make commitments to action for follow-through on decisions
- Make all decisons by majority rule

**HORIZONTAL PROCESS-FOCUSED MEETING BEHAVIORS**

- Ensure full (everyone's) participation*
- Ensure open participation
- Check for understanding
- Focus on the bigger picture
- Explore individual differences
- Ask questions/probe for information
- Think creatively
- Focus on the people
- Look outward for new and different perspectives
- Use a consensus process for making important decisions

* Full participation does not mean that everyone has equal air time. It means that all pertinent ideas, points of view and concerns are expressed.

## TASK/PROCESS MEETING ASSESSMENT

| | Task-Oriented Meeting Behaviors and/or Activities | Process-Oriented Meeting Behaviors and/or Activities |
|---|---|---|
| **Present**<br>*Behaviors demonstrated in the meeting* | | |
| **Missing**<br>*Behaviors that were absent but would have increased the meeting's effectiveness had they been present* | | |

i) Fill in the Task/Process Meeting Assessment form. Put an asterisk beside any behavior that is too strongly demonstrated. Keep in mind that all behaviors are positive and contribute to the group process providing they are suitable to the particular situation and are not demonstrated so strongly as to exclude its opposite pole which provides balance.

ii) Develop agreements to include missing behaviors in future meetings and to moderate those that are too strongly demonstrated.

# CHECK YOUR TEAM'S CLIMATE

**Instructions**

The following team characteristics are team climate indicators. Please rate your team candidly on the scale of 1 to 4 given below.

1-we need a lot of work in this area

4-we are very strong in this area

In order to choose a rating for each Indicator, you may want to consider the questions listed in the Thought Triggers column.

| INDICATOR | THOUGHT TRIGGERS | RATING |
|---|---|---|
| **Openness** | Are team members honest and open with each other? Do people ensure that there are no hidden agendas? Do people feel free to express what they are really thinking? | 1 2 3 4 |
| **Support** | Do team members help each other? Do they support others who make errors without examining the importance of the error? Do they freely help others to perform more effectively? | 1 2 3 4 |
| **Sharing Success** | Do team members take pride in each others' successes? Are they sincerely happy for others' success? Do they look for opportunities to give each other recognition? Do they bring team members' accomplishments to the attention of others? | 1 2 3 4 |
| **Dealing With Conflict** | Does your team deal with small problems before they become issues? Are differences of opinion seen as normal and healthy? Are team members able to separate personalities from the issue at hand? | 1 2 3 4 |
| **Trust** | Do you feel that team members have the team's interest at heart? Do team members have each other's interests at heart? Can you depend on other team members to back you up? To back up the team? | 1 2 3 4 |
| **Team Values** | Do team members hold similar work values? Do they consistently demonstrate these values? | 1 2 3 4 |
| | **Total** | |

# 3

# THE NEW MOVERS
# AND SHAKERS

The new movers and shakers are synthesizers. The synthesizers will shape the new organization. They integrate task and process behaviors to create a new way of working that produces results that are unattainable otherwise. They are able to move comfortably between task and process modes of behaviors. Some will be natural synthesizers; most will have learned to integrate the vertical and the horizontal.

An organization's ability to achieve dynamic balance is influenced by the personal balance of each of its members, and in turn by the members' ability to balance one another's differences. Small individual imbalances can lead to significant organizational imbalances. The effectiveness with which individuals manage the polarities within their personal work styles will determine or at least strongly influence the success of the activities they lead or in which they participate.

There are natural synthesizers who achieve success with the greatest of ease. Everyone knows individuals who strongly favor one dimension of a polarity, such as the highly convergent thinker, for example, who comes into a group decision-making process with his or her mind already made up as to the best decision. Some imbalances are more subtle.

Figure 3.1

## THE TASK/PROCESS DIMENSIONS

| TASK FOCUSED | PROCESS FOCUSED |
|---|---|
| • Independent | • Interactive |
| *Works most effectively when working independently* | *Works most effectively when working with others* |
| • Objective | • Sensitive |
| *Responds with objectivity* | *Responds with sensitivity* |
| • Inward Looking | • Outward Looking |
| *Focuses on details* | *Focuses on the bigger picture* |
| • Logical | • Intuitive |
| *Uses facts and logic* | *Uses creativity and intuition* |
| • Convergent | • Divergent |
| *Brings things to closure* | *Examines possibilities* |

A greater emphasis on the task-focused dimensions results in task behaviors and an emphasis on process-focused dimensions results in process behaviors described on page 32.

*Note: For more detailed descriptions see* Reflection & Application, *pages 56–67.*

# LEARNING TO BE SYNTHESIZERS

Organizations that support members in becoming synthesizers and in understanding the requirements of the new world of work greatly accelerate the emergence of the new organization and increase its chances of success. Cost and distractions prevent many organizations from making a serious commitment to any type of development of its members. North American companies are frequently criticized for not putting sufficient emphasis on the development of their employees.

Japanese auto makers, for example, provide their employees with ten times as much training time as their North American counterparts. Perhaps more important than time is the quality of learning. Too few development programs challenge individuals to reflect, develop self-knowledge and make commitments to action for personal change. Individual balance and personal excellence require introspection and self-knowledge.

As we have discussed, knowledge is our prime resource in the new economy. Peter Drucker, in *Managing in A Time of Great Change*, defines knowledge as "information effective in action, information focused on results." The most important knowledge, and the knowledge that is prerequisite to our ability to use any other knowledge effectively, is self-knowledge.

Outside of the organization, the upheaval of the great transition we are passing through has sparked a quest for self-knowledge. Many people are searching for their spiritual selves and the knowledge of how to tap the best of themselves in every aspect of life by knowing themselves better.

Inside most organizations, however, the focus is on the problem to be solved, the program to be implemented, the team to be built, the customer to be served and the myriad other priorities of every company. How well these priorities are managed, how effectively decisions are made, how they are received and how they are implemented depend on a collection and intermeshing of individual responses. The greater the individual's self-knowledge, the more appropriate the responses (i.e., the better the integration of both task and process behaviors) and the better the outcomes.

## The New Requirements

Self-knowledge requires gathering and analyzing information about oneself and focusing that information on meeting the new organizational requirements. To find their personal balance, members must understand the requirements of the new organization and determine whether their personal task/process balance allows them to meet the new requirements easily.

As we are not yet settled into the new world, all of the requirements may not be clear, but we are quite certain of several. Here is an overview of the essential ones of which every employee must be aware. Under each requirement, I have identified the dimension that best supports it.

## Interconnectedness

Because knowledge is becoming the prime resource, it is essential that individuals' knowledge pieces be appropriately connected to achieve the purpose of their organization. Teamwork may take place in formal teams made up of a group of individuals whose different knowledge sets come together to complete a specific task. Teamwork may also take place informally as individuals come together spontaneously as needed to share, interpret and apply information.

If knowledge is the resource, interconnectedness is the system that brings the pieces of knowledge together in insightful and creative ways to produce superior results.

The interconnectedness is as important as the knowledge itself. Individuals' ability to work effectively in teams and to connect formally and informally will determine the degree to which they can contribute to the organization.

Task/Process Dimension — *Interactive*

## Information Gathering and Continuous Learning

In the new organization, each individual is required to keep abreast of the constant changes in his or her knowledge area. Each person must gather pertinent information, interpret it and apply it. The new organization requires all of its members to be environmental scanners. They must be experts and keep up in their area of expertise, and at the same time be well-informed generalists. To use their expertise, they must connect with many other areas and make decisions based on a fast-changing world. Therefore, a broad knowledge base is important. Being able to gather all of the needed information, of course, requires the ability to use technology.

The new worker must be able to shift personal paradigms, to look at things from a different perspective that will lead to new and perhaps less comfortable conclusions.

Task/Process Dimensions — *Outward Looking and Divergent*

## Creative Thinking

People must be able to engage in creative thinking. Edward de Bono, who coined the term "lateral thinking," describes our traditional vertical thinking as digging the same hole deeper. Lateral thinking, he suggests, is digging a new hole somewhere else. The new organization requires people who are able to dig new holes in unusual places.

Task/Process Dimension — *Intuitive*

## Risk Taking

Digging new holes somewhere else also requires some risk taking. We are in a world made for pioneers, a world full of endless possibilities where few things are certain. Organizations need people who are willing to make what might appear to be outlandish suggestions and try new and not yet proven approaches.

Task/Process Dimensions — *Intuitive and to some extent Divergent*

### Seeing the Big Picture

We will continue to require members to make more decisions independently. To make decisions that are valuable not just to their own immediate area but to the organization as a whole, individuals must be able to see each decision in the context of the bigger picture.

Task/Process Dimension — *Outward Looking*

### Self-Assessment and Personal Change

Perhaps the most important requirement is the courage to examine one's self honestly, welcome feedback and make adjustments as required. Defensive individuals will close themselves off from the input needed for growth, will atrophy and die in relation to the organization.

The new organization will continuously evolve. Members must evolve with it.

Task/Process Dimensions — *Divergent and Intuitive*

# MAKING THE ADJUSTMENTS

Individuals' success will be based not only on their natural profile, but on their ability to make adjustments as required. There is a great deal of emphasis on being able to cope in the new economy, but "coping" suggests getting by rather than being highly successful. One can cope without making any personal change or adjusting to the new world, at least for a short while. Those who will be able to work with the greatest ease will have developed a synchronicity with the new ways of work. These individuals will have made adjustments. Individuals who do not have a natural task/process balance (who are not synthesizers) can learn compensating behaviors. They can also make a point of working with, and listening to, team members who have a preference for opposite dimensions. If we are not balanced as individuals, we can achieve balance through teamwork.

# THEORY IN ACTION

## Impact of Task/Process Balance on Leadership Effectiveness

Consider the example of the team-based manufacturing plant that I described in the last chapter.

John was the plant manager. He was frustrated when, after several months, the teams were not meeting expectations. Management was still carrying on with tasks and making decisions they believed should be made by the teams. The increased drive and energy that had initially been created did not have staying power and some important production targets had not been met.

John recognized that the teams were struggling but he thought that the problem belonged to other people. He prided himself on being a motivator. He regularly reminded the plant's team leaders of the company's mission and liked to share colorful examples that made a point. He had been keen when their CEO put the team concept in place. He felt he would be able to motivate the new team leaders to create the teams and outcomes that had been envisioned. He soon became frustrated, however, by what he saw as lack of initiative on the part of the leaders. The teams seldom responded to his requests for action without his follow-up. Also, important information was not being passed on to team members.

Management knew that teams were essential if the organization was to be successful in a competitive and changing environment. John worried that the leaders might not have what it would take to make the self-directed team concept work.

---

### JOHN'S TASK/PROCESS PROFILE

| TASK | PROCESS |
|---|---|
| Independent | — |
| — | Sensitive |
| — | Outward Looking |
| — | Intuitive |
| Convergent | — |

---

When he examined his personal task/process balance (using the questionnaire, pages 56–62), he identified his personal preferences and realized that they influenced his leadership of the self-directed team process. Some of his process orientation, Outward Looking and Intuitive, had supported him in dealing with change and working comfortably in the new world of work. However, he found that three of his dimensions were exceptionally strong and therefore out of balance. He realized that these strong behavioral preferences contributed to the problem that he had attributed to others.

His very strong sensitive dimension revealed his emotional nature. He had demonstrated this dimension positively in his enthusiasm for the new team concept; he had been excited about what he had believed could be achieved. However, his sensitivity was also reflected in the strong feeling of disappointment he had experienced when the leaders did not live up to his expectations. He had felt they had let him down, personally, and he had not objectively examined the situation.

As a highly convergent thinker, he had strong ideas of right and wrong, and he was not easily swayed from a position. Once he had made up his mind that the leaders were not taking responsibility, it was difficult for them to convince him otherwise. At times, he had not noticed their responsible actions because he had seen only what fit into his indelible picture of their irresponsibility. There would have had to be a drastic change for him to have altered his perspective. He assumed his reasoning was correct and had not listened when team members tried to explain their difficulty in living up to some of the expectations.

John found his outward focus to be most revealing. He recognized that his lack of detail orientation meant that he often threw out general requests or broad pieces of information to the leaders. He did not provide sufficient specifics, such as who, what, why, where or when. The lack of specifics also meant that a sense of urgency was lacking. This resulted in particular difficulties in communicating with the leaders, who were almost all highly inward looking with a strong need for detail. He was not providing what they needed, particularly while they were adjusting to new roles and were in a learning mode. John made a commitment to communicating more clearly and specifically. He also realized that as the leaders continued their development process, one of their needs would be to balance their high level of detail orientation with a more outward, bigger-picture focus.

John's personal balance did not match the group's needs at this stage of its development. Were the group of leaders further developed, he would not have had to provide them with as much structure and his style would have worked more effectively.

Had his inward-looking/outward-looking dimensions been better integrated, he would have instinctively known when to provide specifics and when to throw out general requests. Recognizing his imbalance reminded him to give more specific instructions, even though that wasn't his natural tendency.

Imbalances in John's style were, of course, not the only factor contributing to the team's mediocre performance, but because of his role, they were a major one. The team leaders' assessment of their personal balance also indicated to them changes they needed to make in order to meet the requirements better in the new workplace.

In most cases, individuals are able to express both poles of a dimension if they make a conscious and consistent effort to do so.

## Impact of a Member's Task/Process Preference on a Team

The Product Management Team had not been able to come to agreement on the launch of a new product. The team thought that consensus had finally been reached, and the group was ready to move on to other things. However, one of the members, Tracy, sent a memo requesting another meeting. To the group's surprise, she presented a very different recommendation at the meeting. She very briefly said she had some serious concerns about the logic behind the last decision and felt that there were important issues that had been overlooked.

The group was frustrated and angry. Why hadn't she raised the points earlier? In addition, there was a sense that Tracy had a tendency to be secretive, and people were beginning to wonder about hidden agendas and ulterior motives, particularly as a lot of restructuring was happening in the organization. They wondered whether there was a power struggle going on.

| TRACY'S TASK/PROCESS PROFILE | |
|---|---|
| **TASK** | **PROCESS** |
| Independent | — |
| Objective | — |
| Inward Looking | — |
| Logical | Intuitive |
| Convergent | — |

### Independent Tendencies

On reviewing her profile, Tracy recognized that her strength was not in working in groups but working independently. She did her best work thinking on her own. The group process inhibited her thinking, and when decisions were made in a session, her later solitary reflection would often bring forward concerns that she had not thought of in the meeting.

She communicated better in writing than in person and so she relied on memos and e-mail. In retrospect, she realized this, and also, she discovered that her tendency to use formal language created the impression she was sending edicts rather than ideas or suggestions. Because she didn't talk about ideas before formalizing them, she was seen as secretive or suspected of "cooking up" something. She also did not think to communicate with others and therefore sometimes did not pass along information others saw as important, or didn't always check with others on decisions that affected them.

### Inward-Looking and Logical Tendencies

Tracy saw that she was highly logical and had a need for detail. Although these qualities had often served her well in the past, she saw that in discussions she had missed the bigger picture. Some ideas that she had mentally rejected because her store of knowledge did not support them actually were important and probably very creative.

Tracy's examination of her profile allowed her to recognize areas in which she needed to adjust her behavior in order to function more effectively in the new world of work. Sharing her profile with her colleagues also gave them a better understanding of why she behaved the way she did. Her team members also had an opportunity to look at their profiles and recognized ways in which they could support her in being more effective.

## REFLECTION & APPLICATION

The following personal Task/Process Balance Assessment can be used to help determine one's present balance, and to recognize strengths and opportunities for growth.

## PERSONAL TASK/PROCESS BALANCE ASSESSMENT

Each individual has his or her own task/process orientation. Answer the following questions to identify your own. There are no "right" answers.

Base your response to the statements on how you prefer to work, or what comes most naturally to you. The higher the rating, the stronger your preference.

Rate both (a) and (b) statements: (a) and (b) must add up to 5 in any combination.

    e.g.    (a) 2    (b) 3
            (a) 1    (b) 4
            (a) 5    (b) 0

Each rating must be a whole number.

1. (a) To reenergize, I prefer quiet time alone.

    Score _____

   (b) To reenergize, I prefer to be active with other people.

    Score _____

2. (a) In meetings, my focus is on the information being discussed.

    Score _____

   (b) In meetings, I am very aware of people's reactions and body language.

    Score _____

3. (a) I prefer to focus on theory.

    Score _____

   (b) I prefer to focus on task/ application.

    Score _____

4. (a) I prefer to be "doing."

    Score _____

   (b) I prefer to be "thinking."

    Score _____

5. (a) I push for closure on issues.

    Score _____

   (b) I let closure happen when the group is ready.

    Score _____

6. (a) I develop my best ideas brainstorming with others.

    Score _____

   (b) I develop my best ideas reflecting on my own.

    Score _____

7. (a) I like to be recognized for my critical-thinking abilities.

Score _____

(b) I like to be recognized for my empathy.

Score _____

8. (a) I find developing goals and objectives satisfying.

Score _____

(b) I find working on missions, visions and values statements satisfying.

Score _____

9. (a) I prefer soving problems in a step-by-step fashion.

Score _____

(b) I prefer solving problems by brainstorming for solutions.

Score _____

10. (a) I prefer knowing what to expect.

Score _____

(b) I prefer dealing with the unexpected.

Score _____

11. (a) I solve problems by looking to others for their experience/input.

Score _____

(b) I solve problems by drawing on my own experience.

Score _____

12. (a) I am influenced by inspirational, motivated individuals who speak with emotion.

Score _____

(b) I am influenced by individuals who present their case rationally, supported by concrete examples or data.

Score _____

13. (a) When faced with a problem, my first instinct is to analyze the problem, the causes and its implications.

Score _____

(b) When faced with a problem, my first instinct is to generate solutions.

Score _____

14. (a) I prefer being recognized for my creativity.

Score _____

(b) I prefer being recognized for my logic.

Score _____

15. (a) I easily see others' points of view.

Score _____

(b) I have firm beliefs about right and wrong or what will work and what won't.

Score _____

16. (a) I prefer working through issues and problems on my own and then passing on my thoughts.

Score _____

(b) I prefer working through issues in a group.

Score _____

17. (a) I work toward the best solution, even if it may not be supported by everyone.

Score _____

(b) I work toward the solution that can best be supported by the group.

Score _____

18. (a) I read broadly.

Score _____

(b) I read material pertaining to my own industry/area of expertise.

Score _____

19. (a) I prefer trying something new.

Score _____

(b) I prefer using methods that have worked for me before.

Score _____

20. (a) I prefer carefully gathering and considering all information before making decisions.

Score _____

(b) I prefer making decisions quickly based on information at hand.

Score _____

21. (a) It seldom occurs to me to share information about what I am doing unless asked.

Score _____

(b) I enjoy sharing information about what I am doing and look for opportunities to do so.

Score _____

22. (a) I make decisions based on my beliefs and feelings.

Score _____

(b) I make decisions based on facts and figures.

Score _____

23. (a) I prefer to focus on the detail.    (b) I prefer to focus on the idea.

         Score \_\_\_\_\_                 Score \_\_\_\_\_

24. (a) I prefer thinking about what    (b) I prefer dealing with what is.
could be.

         Score \_\_\_\_\_                 Score \_\_\_\_\_

25. (a) I prefer working to plan.    (b) I prefer working according to
needs as they arise.

         Score \_\_\_\_\_                 Score \_\_\_\_\_

26. (a) I enjoy talking with others about   (b) In conversation, I prefer talking
my experiences and successes.    about others rather than myself.

         Score \_\_\_\_\_                 Score \_\_\_\_\_

27. (a) I judge people on their    (b) I judge people on the outcomes
intentions.    they produce.

         Score \_\_\_\_\_                 Score \_\_\_\_\_

28. (a) I enjoy responsibilities that    (b) I find dealing with detail
require attention to detail.    tedious.

         Score \_\_\_\_\_                 Score \_\_\_\_\_

29. (a) My decisions are strongly    (b) My decisions are strongly
influenced by facts and figures.    influenced by my sense of
what is best.

         Score \_\_\_\_\_                 Score \_\_\_\_\_

30. (a) I like to stick to a schedule.    (b) I prefer to use schedules as
general guidelines to be
changed as needed.

         Score \_\_\_\_\_                 Score \_\_\_\_\_

## PERSONAL TASK/PROCESS BALANCE SCORING SHEET

Transfer your scores for each statement to the appropriate spaces below.
**Note:** Record your scores *carefully*. At times, the (a)'s and (b)'s are reversed.

### Independent

1.  (a) _____
6.  (b) _____
11. (b) _____
16. (a) _____
21. (a) _____
26. (b) _____

**Total** _____

### Interactive

1.  (b) _____
6.  (a) _____
11. (a) _____
16. (b) _____
21. (b) _____
26. (a) _____

**Total** _____

### Objective

2.  (a) _____
7.  (a) _____
12. (b) _____
17. (a) _____
22. (b) _____
27. (b) _____

**Total** _____

### Sensitive

2.  (b) _____
7.  (b) _____
12. (a) _____
17. (b) _____
22. (a) _____
27. (a) _____

**Total** _____

### Inward Looking

3.  (b) _____
8.  (a) _____

13. (b) _____
18. (b) _____
23. (a) _____
28. (a) _____

**Total** _____

### Outward Looking

3.  (a) _____
8.  (b) _____

13. (a) _____
18. (a) _____
23. (b) _____
28. (b) _____

**Total** _____

## Logical

4.   (a) _____
9.   (a) _____
14.  (b) _____
19.  (b) _____
24.  (b) _____
29.  (a) _____

## Total _____

## Intuitive

4.   (b) _____
9.   (b) _____
14.  (a) _____
19.  (a) _____
24.  (a) _____
29.  (b) _____

## Total _____

## Convergent

5.   (a) _____
10.  (a) _____
15.  (b) _____
20.  (b) _____
25.  (a) _____
30.  (a) _____

## Total _____

## Divergent

5.   (b) _____
10.  (b) _____
15.  (a) _____
20.  (a) _____
25.  (b) _____
30.  (b) _____

## Total _____

Please transfer your totals to the balance profile below.

## PERSONAL TASK/PROCESS BALANCE PROFILE

| TASK FOCUSED | | PROCESS FOCUSED | |
| --- | --- | --- | --- |
| Independent | _____ | Interactive | _____ |
| Objective | _____ | Sensitive | _____ |
| Inward Looking | _____ | Outward Looking | _____ |
| Logical | _____ | Intuitive | _____ |
| Convergent | _____ | Divergent | _____ |
| Total | _____ | Total | _____ |

## INTERPRETATION

The personal profile describes an individual's most comfortable and most natural style. If one pole of a dimension is dominant, the individual brings to the organization particular strengths in that area. Too much strength in any pole, however, results in weakness in its opposite pole, which may handicap the individual and the organization. Not all characteristics presented under each pole in the dimension descriptions will apply unless the individual strongly favors that pole.

### Dimension Scores

If a score ranges from 14 to 16 for each pole of a dimension, the individual can probably work comfortably across the dimension and move back and forth between the poles as appropriate.

A score of 17+ indicates a preferred pole. A preferred pole describes the way in which the individual works most comfortably and therefore most easily. It does not mean that the individual is unable to demonstrate the other pole of the dimension; however, he or she probably has to be reminded to do so. The greater the difference between the scores of the two poles of a dimension (e.g., Independent-Interactive), the greater the difficulty in demonstrating the behaviors associated with the weaker pole.

### Total Scores

A Task score of 80+ suggests a Task orientation.

A Process score of 80+ suggests a Process orientation.

A score ranging from Task 70 to Process 80 or Task 80 to Process 70 suggests the individual is a synthesizer, one who moves comfortably and appropriately between task focus and process focus. Synthesizers meet the expectations of the new world of work more easily than others.

### Task/Process Dimension Descriptions

#### Independent/Interactive

*Independent*

Individuals who show a preference for the independent mode:
• Work best independently;
• Can be disadvantaged in group work — they often develop ideas best

by thinking quietly on their own, and a group discussion can block rather than stimulate their thinking;
- Often do not think of communicating with others as they do not have a strong need to interact with others — because they do not share information readily, they can be misunderstood and seen as hoarding information, being secretive or aloof;
- Do not necessarily want to retreat to a cabin in the woods but do look to solitary activities to reenergize.

### Interactive

Individuals who show a preference for the interactive mode:
- Need people around them and reenergize by being active with others. Work best with others;
- Need interaction to stimulate their thought processes. They thrive on meetings, think well out loud and may dominate discussion. They regularly create their own meetings by carrying a coffee into another's office to bounce ideas off her or him. It does not occur to them that they might be disturbing someone because any intrusion in their day is a welcomed relief;
- Need variety.

## Objective/Sensitive

### Objective

Individuals who have a preference for the objective mode:
- Are able to stand back emotionally from issues and examine them with detachment — they separate facts from emotion and use the facts; they recognize and test assumptions;
- Can miss people factors;
- Do not value opinions that are not proven by fact;
- Take pride in being sensible and level headed;
- Others' opinions of them are not of great concern to them.

### Sensitive

Individuals who have a preference for the sensitive mode:
- Become emotionally involved in issues;
- Are aware of and consider others' feelings;
- Are more strongly influenced by feelings than logic;

• Are moved by emotional pleas or motivational presentations;
• Create energy and enthusiasm for ideas they support;
• Show emotion.

### Inward Looking/Outward Looking

*Inward Looking*

Individuals who have a preference for the inward-looking mode:
• Work well with detail and see it easily and clearly — they can get caught up dotting i's and crossing t's and miss the bigger picture;
• Focus on the job at hand;
• Like to have clear goals and objectives;
• Like structure;
• Tend to focus on their particular area of expertise and not to develop broad interests or become a generalist.

*Outward Looking*

Individuals with a preference for the outward-looking mode:
• Are tuned into the bigger picture;
• Can be frustrated by detail people;
• Speak in broad terms and generalities;
• Would prefer developing a mission statement or strategic plan to developing goals and objectives;
• Enjoy exploring the theory behind an application and the cause and effect of issues;
• Value being well-versed in many topics.

### Logical/Intuitive

*Logical*

Individuals who prefer the logical mode:
• Need the world to make sense — they like to approach things in a logical step-by-step fashion;
• Believe things and issues can be easily resolved with a little common sense, and to them issues are black or white;
• Prefer to work with structured models when problem solving. Wide open brainstorming or "blue skying" does not appeal;
• Prefer a structured work environment.

*Intuitive*

Individuals with a preference for the intuitive mode:

• Like to think and explore possibilities;

• Are not limited by a need for structure or preconceived ideas;

• Are open to all possibilities;

• Like to try new approaches;

• Like to brainstorm;

• Generate creative ideas;

• Are not comfortable working in a highly structured environment or mode;

• Often examine issues from different, and not apparently logical, perspectives;

• Are more likely to take what appear to be risks as they choose a decision they "feel good" about, but which may not be supported by logic.

## Convergent/Divergent

*Convergent*

Individuals with a preference for the convergent mode:

• Have very firm opinions;

• Live comfortably with their decisions feeling confident that they are right;

• Are quick to make decisions and change their mind very reluctantly;

• Become impatient with any discussion they see as wheel spinning;

• Like to work to plan;

• Often play the role of moving things to closure;

• Are likely to supply answers — to tell, rather than ask questions.

*Divergent*

Individuals with a preference for the divergent mode:

• Like to hear as much information as possible;

• Are open to others' points of view;

• Carefully consider all information and opinions;

• Like a discussion to run its own course and to reach closure when the group is ready;

• Take a facilitative approach to dealing with people, asking rather than telling;

• Enjoy working with the unexpected and dealing with needs as they arise;

• Look for compromise.

**Individual Activity**

On completion of the Personal Task/Process Balance questionnaire, complete your personal profile and then examine it in context of the requirements in the new place of work: interconnectedness, information gathering and continuous learning, creative thinking, risk taking and seeing the big picture.

Examine each of your dimensions and determine which will best support you in meeting each of the requirements and any of those that may hinder you in working effectively in the new world of work.

# Part II

# BECOMING WISE

Wisdom is the result of basing
the application of information on
an intuitive understanding of the
information, of one's self, and of
the nature of the world in which it
will be applied.

# 4

# OWLS, SAGES AND LEADERSHIP

It has been the era of the corporate action hero — the leader with quick reflexes, corporate street smarts and aggressive confidence. Cool-handed under pressure, this hero can make quick, tough and sometimes risky decisions, and rally the troops to carry them out.

The action heroes have downsized, refocused, restructured and reengineered. They have been able to examine the facts, deduce the possible outcomes, select the most favorable course of action and put it in motion. They have been able to pick up and customize others' good ideas. They have taken organizations apart and stitched them back together. Those who have succeeded have created well-oiled, more efficient machines that should be capable of the responsiveness required in the new economy.

Will these highly intelligent, rational achievers be able to take the organization the next step into the new economy? Are they able to provide the wisdom to arrive at the less obvious solutions and make the more intuitive decisions that will determine vitality in the new economy? Are they able to look inward and create the required individualized homemade models for success? Can the action hero also be wise?

Some, of course, are. Jack Welch at GE is an obvious example of an action hero. He came into GE and quickly reshaped the business and the organization. His recognition that the new GE would succeed only if driven by a culture of empowerment, and his persistence in creating one, suggest wisdom. What GE did in the 1980s — create a responsive culture in sync with the new economy — many companies have just begun.

Many got to this point without wisdom, relying on vertical reasoning and quick decision making. The ever more ephemeral world requires wisdom. Wisdom combines reason, action and intuition. Wisdom is the application of knowledge based on an intuitive sense of self and the world around us. Organizational wisdom is the application of knowledge based on an intuitive sense of the organization and the world within which it operates.

*In all cultures, the wise person is one who is able to make the right decision in circumstances in which reason alone is inadequate.*

John Dalla Costa
*Working Wisdom*

Throughout time and across cultures, wisdom has been revered. It is considered to be the highest level of intelligence, and to have wisdom or to receive the counsel of the wise is much desired. To live wisely means to live without exhausting ourselves through struggle; to find the best way, not the mediocre way.

Yet in the corporate world, wisdom has received little notice. The highly vertical Newtonian organization has lauded reason and logic. The concept of wisdom does not fit into a box or equation and therefore did not have a place in the traditional organization. Since organizations got by and sometimes were very successful with logic-based decisions in a more concrete, slower-paced world, the need for wisdom was not as apparent.

As organizations tire of the struggle and find that logic is not enough, the search for wisdom has begun. How do people attain wisdom? The word "wisdom" sparks images of owls and sages, both old, peaceful, solitary and contemplative. Some studies suggest that there actually is a relationship between age and wisdom. German researcher Paul Baltes found that, in testing for wisdom, half of the wisest responses came from subjects over the age of 60.

It has already been recognized that the flood of early retirement packages taken in the 1990s to lessen the human-resource cost burden has depleted some organizations of a large percentage of their knowledge reservoir. If there is a correlation between age and wisdom, the long-term loss may be greater than current estimates.

Deepak Chopra quotes Jonas Salk on wisdom: "It's something that you know when you see it. You can recognize it, you can experience it. I have defined wisdom as the capacity to make judgments that when looked back upon will seem to have been wise." Based on this definition, one could say that all classic business success stories, whether McDonald's, Apple, Microsoft or Wal-Mart, are based on wise decisions by their entrepreneurial founders.

Wisdom is not only required in recognizing opportunities or making strategic decisions, but on a day-to-day, moment-to-moment basis as well. De-layering and empowerment have led to knowledge-based organizations, composed mostly of self-directed individuals, resulting in environments that require wisdom throughout the organization. Wisdom requires information plus intuition.

Thomas Ouchi's *The Z Organization* examines features in some North American organizations that resemble Japanese firms. He comments on the traditional lack of balance between logic and intuition in the Western organization: "Western management seems to be characterized for the most part by an ethos which roughly runs as follows: rational is better than non-rational, objective is more nearly rational than subjective, quantitative is more objective than non-quantitative and thus quantitative analysis is preferred over judgments based on wisdom, experience and subtlety.

"In a type Z company the explicit and the implicit seem to exist in a state of balance."

> Wisdom emerges when there is a task/process balance.

The need for increased wisdom suggests new opportunities for individuals who may have been overlooked in the traditional organization. Outgoing, assertive, verbal individuals have had the "influencing advantage." As the need for greater wisdom becomes recognized, quieter, more contemplative thinkers will become more appreciated. One challenge for organizations is to learn how to tap the wisdom that lies dormant.

# TAPPING WISDOM

Wisdom in an organization requires information about current events and ideas, within and without, plus insight about the organization and the world with which it interacts. Individuals can no longer keep sufficiently in tune independently. No one individual can be the retainer of all pertinent information. Exchanging information, ideas and insights can spark wisdom. We know that the most profound new insights tend to be made at the edges, not at the center of an area of specialty. Linking specialists and nonspecialists can trigger innovative thinking. Interconnectedness is essential.

### Making the Connection
Group processes, essential to self-direction and interconnectedness, can stifle wisdom. Too much talk, or too little reflection, is not conducive to wisdom. Interconnectedness that is essential to wisdom can also stifle wisdom.

Independent thinkers — those who develop their best ideas thinking quietly in a corner — are often disadvantaged in these verbal sessions. Well-managed group processes ensure equal opportunities for all thinking styles. Wisdom emerges when the task/process dimensions are in balance.

### On Reflection
The action-oriented organization denies time for reflection. The wise organization recognizes that reflection time is a basic need — a few moments of staring off into space is not considered nonproductive time.

In the action-oriented meeting, if a group decision is postponed to a future meeting, the group is spinning its wheels. In the wise organization, important decisions are taken in a three-part process. Part one is the sharing of information and dialogue to shape the body of knowledge pertaining to the decision at hand. Part two is a brief gestation period — this could be sending people away to think about it overnight or moving individuals to quiet corners to reflect for 10 minutes (very important decisions might warrant longer periods of reflection). Part three is a sharing of any further insights through dialogue, discussing the body of knowledge that has been created by the group (weighing the pros and cons) and making a decision (see Figure 4.1).

Figure 4.1

---

## MAKING WISE DECISIONS

Part 1    Sharing of Information and Dialoguing
Part 2    Gestation Period (reflection time)
Part 3    Further Dialogue → Discussion → Decision

---

Wisdom allows individuals to work within chaos rather than waste energy trying to control chaos. It allows them to get in flow with change around them.

In chapter 1, I referred to Edward Lorenz's popularized butterfly effect: the flutter of a butterfly's wings in China can create turbulence in New York the next month. It illustrates the heightened need for wisdom in the new economy. When a system is not in equilibrium, small changes in input to the system (the flutter of the butterfly's wings) can produce large changes in outcome. Wisdom is required to recognize the importance of the event. This means understanding the event and the system in which the event is taking place, how that event will play out, considering all of the variables. In the organizational world this is not a mathematical computation, but an intuitive sense of what is happening and its short- and long-term implications.

An article in the January 1975 issue of *Popular Electronics* on a kit for a mini-computer, the Altaire 8800, was a flutter of a butterfly's wings. Bill Gates intuitively understood its meaning; he understood the larger context that technology would not just provide data for organizations, but information for people. People at IBM must have seen the article as well, but did not immediately comprehend the turbulence it would create in their mainframe world.

Socrates believed that wisdom could not be taught but only known directly. Wisdom, however, is information plus intuition. Information can be learned and intuition can be developed.

# 5

# BEING INFORMED: THE NEXT CORPORATE VALUE

My first recognition of what information was and the excitement it held was at about the age of eight when I discovered a very old set of encyclopedias that had belonged to my father's family when he was a child. Probably published in the 1920s or early 30s, the books were bound in blue-black leather, had somewhat musty and yellow pages with a few black-and-white photos and were housed in their own small bookcase.

I was sure that everything there was to know in the whole world was collected between those few covers (it didn't occur to me that much of the information was 30 years out of date). I was soon on imaginary archaeological digs in Egypt, and on safari through the densest jungles of Africa.

My children, with the click of the mouse, have more information available to them in their CD-ROM encyclopedia than that little bookshelf could have held. They access not just copy and black-and-white pictures, but sound, color photos, referenced articles and even video clips. Everything they need and information leading them to more information they wouldn't even have thought of searching out slip onto the screen in an easy-to-understand and enticing format. The down side is that they may not be exercising their imagination and creativity to the extent that I had to.

In 1951, there were approximately ten thousand journals compared to the one hundred and forty thousand listed today in *Ulrich's International Periodicals Directory*. The accessibility of information is not the new organization's challenge; technology has taken care of that and will continue to find ways to provide even easier access to even more specific information. Technology increases the amount of information to which we have access, and at the same time makes it easier for us to target the information we need, helping to prevent information overload. The need for usable information, however, does present many issues that require attention.

The first challenge is knowing what information is required. The second is developing our awareness of the need to constantly update our own individual information base as well as our skills in gathering and applying the information.

Most organizations have put effort into incorporating the values of quality, customer service, empowerment and teamwork into the corporate culture. The values of quality and customer service have been embraced with a great deal of success. There has been substantive change as a result. Less success so far has been experienced in making empowerment and effective teamwork part of the organizational fiber. These two values still require more work in most organizations.

In addition, there is now considerable urgency to incorporate information as the new organizational value. Few organizations have given any serious thought to information as an organizational value and yet the effective use of information will make or break the organization in the new economy. The importance of information is not likely to be a surprise to anyone since we are moving into what is frequently referred to as the information age. In addition, we know that the pace of change is not decelerating, and therefore we know that more information will continue to be required in order to keep up with the change, and more and more information will be produced. Yet information has not been embraced as a value and few organizations are putting initiatives in place to ensure that they have the information they need to function in the new world. Without critical current information, a company will be flying by the seat of its pants and the seat will wear out very quickly.

# OUTWARD-LOOKING ORGANIZATIONS

Having ready access to external information is critical during dynamic times. It requires that we become more outward looking. For years Peter Drucker has emphasized the need to be outward looking. As he has repeatedly pointed out, results happen outside of the organization. That is where the connections are made that create the results. It makes sense, then, that we know what's going on out there. That sense helped draw companies to the value of superior customer service. Soon everybody wanted to know how well we liked them. We couldn't eat in a restaurant, stay in a hotel, fly in a plane or walk through a mall without being asked our opinion on products and service. In fact, companies were so determined to please customers by getting their input that they often inconvenienced them to get it. "Please, sir. I know you are in a hurry, but your opinion is very valuable to us."

Organizations realized that they must look outside for information, but they stopped with the customer. The customer's input has been valuable in helping companies improve but it is not nearly far reaching enough. What about the reason the rest of the population are not customers, or what about the competitor's successful and not-so-successful activities and direction? What about the potentially new competitors, the new directions and technology in our industry, the global economy, international politics, and on and on? As part of a system whose ability to change has been greatly accelerated by technology, there will be little that is not in some way relevant to an organization in the twenty-first century. Information needs to be distilled, but aggregate information can be so distilled that it loses any meaning.

*Where is the Life we have lost in living?*
*Where is the wisdom we have lost in knowledge?*
*Where is the knowledge we have lost in information?*

T.S. Eliot
*Choruses from "The Rock"*

We could add the line,
*Where is the information we have lost in data?*

How can we distill the enormous amount of data spinning about us, glean the bits (or mounds) that are most directly pertinent to us and interpret them in such a way that they become usable information? This is the question that organizations must answer.

The company that succeeds in the new economy will be in a permanent state of evolution as it adjusts to stay in sync with the constantly changing world. It will be highly responsive. But responsiveness requires current information that is so well integrated into the organization's system that its application is instinctive and intuitive.

Therefore, all members of the organization must become outward-looking, environmental scanners. Scanners, in particular the knowledge workers, become the organization's nerve ends who instantaneously collect information, and transmit to the appropriate nerve center interpreted messages, along with directions for the required response. Environmental scanners need to work much like money managers who constantly watch the market, economic, political and industry changes and adjust their portfolios accordingly. They need to be dipping into the information soup at least once a day and spooning up the important bits, sharing the bits or an interpretation of them, and together sensing trends and making adjustments (see Figure 5.1).

The need for information scanning throughout the organization, not just at the planning level, is tied closely to the needs of the knowledge-based organization. Workers will be increasingly self-directed and they will not only direct their day-to-day activities but will influence the shape and direction of the organization. This trend will be particularly true of the knowledge workers, whose degree of specialty will necessitate their working in a self-directed mode. The quality of their knowledge will determine the success of the organization. These workers, in particular, must become eager and effective environmental scanners. Organizations must ensure that time is dedicated to gathering information and that members are held accountable for doing so.

Not long ago, meetings, task forces and participation were considered optional. People participated if they "felt like it." In most organizations, it is now clear that participating in and contributing to not just one's own area of responsibility but the organization at large is part of the job. The same must happen with environmental scanning.

Figure 5.1

## ENVIRONMENTAL SCANNING

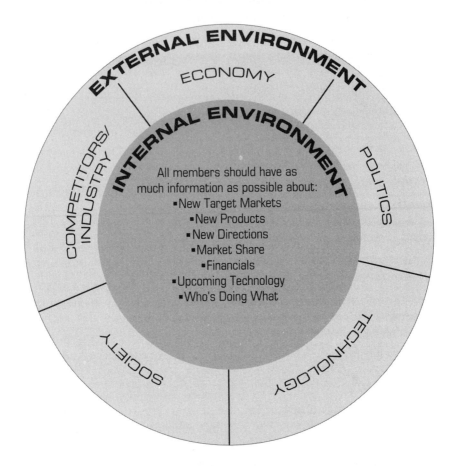

Workers will gather information pertaining to their specialty to ensure that their knowledge is current — but they will do more than that. In order to make decisions in the new economy, one must have expertise in a particular area, but at the same time have a broad understanding of the world within which the decision is being made. This requires being attuned to variables — small disruptions in patterns and anomalies in the various areas that impact the environment in which the decision will be applied. These are the ripples that suggest future change and opportunities on which those most in tune will capitalize.

Information gathered, then, is for several purposes:
• To keep scanners up-to-date in their specialty;
• To ensure they are broadly informed so as to allow for quality decision making on a day-to-day basis;
• To provide information to the organization that will allow it to be in sync with the world and make the appropriate strategic decisions.

Planners will also become increasingly eclectic in their information gathering. Royal Dutch/Shell was one of the first corporations, if not the first, to understand the importance of information, but also the importance of developing models for integrating the information in organizational responses. In the early seventies, the planners at Royal Dutch/Shell gathered pieces of information that they recognized were likely to affect the price of oil, which had been relatively steady since World War II.

Peter Schwartz in *The Art of the Long View* describes the information that was identified as critical: "First the U.S. was beginning to exhaust its oil reserves. Meanwhile, America's demand for oil was steadily rising and the emerging Organization of Petroleum Exporting Countries was showing signs of flexing its political muscle. Most of these countries were Islamic and they bitterly resented Western support of Israel after the 1967 six day Arab-Israeli war."

The planners realized that the Arabs could demand much higher prices for their oil. It was likely they would. They shared their information with the organization but no change in behavior came. Pierre Wack, one of the planners facing the dilemma of how to transmit the integration of information into behavior, developed scenarios that created real pictures that made people feel the possible oil-price shocks. They worked. When the energy crisis hit the world in 1973, only Shell was prepared for the change and took off to eventually challenge Exxon for first place in the global oil industry.

Gathering information is critical but knowing how to use it effectively is just as important. Organizations that will have and will use the information that they need will know what information is required; will have made information scanning part of the job; will know how to integrate information into organizational responses; and will share internal information — including strategic information — and good and bad news quickly and openly.

External information cannot be used in a vacuum. Not only must the organization scan the external environment but it must have internal systems that allow internal information to be accessed easily. Without this internal information it would be impossible for people to weigh the importance of the external information they scan.

Henry Mintzberg cautions organizations not to forget their "soft information." Everyone has access to the soft information — facial expression, body language, tone of voice, anecdotal information and general observations that can communicate information that may be more important than the data. Many people, often the highly task oriented, are oblivious to the soft information or give it less value than the data because it is not quantitative. Training oneself to be attuned to the soft information can greatly improve the decision-making track record. If we are not sensitive to subtle information, we must at least make ourselves listen to those who are. We must look for the soft information clues when gathering both internal and external information.

*Overall, in our opinion, while hard data may inform the intellect, it is largely soft data that generates wisdom.*

Henry Mintzberg
*The Rise and Fall of Strategic Planning*

# INCREASING THE VALUE OF INFORMATION THROUGH SHARING

In the traditional organization, information was power and power was hoarded. In the new organization, information is power and becomes more powerful when shared and applied. The importance of interconnectedness becomes more obvious in the context of information sharing and application. The effectiveness of teamwork in the new organization will directly affect the value of the information collected.

The spontaneous sharing of information is also important and will depend on the ease with which it can be shared and the motivation to share it. Information is most likely to be spontaneously shared when:

• The sharing of information is a demonstrated corporate value;

• Technology allows easy sharing of information;

• Physical layout is conducive to spontaneous sharing. For example, circular office layouts with a communal central area reminiscent of the old town square create interaction.

# INFORMATION FROM WITHIN

Generating information from within for our own and others' use is equally important. Pausing to examine what we have been doing, how we have been doing it, what has worked and what has not, and sharing this information with others is critical to success.

Most people have been brought up in environments in which being right is rewarded and declaring one's errors has few incentives attached to it. People are willing to self-examine and acknowledge weaknesses or mistakes only in an environment in which mistakes are seen as learning opportunities. Without this continuous learning process, we will not be able to use to full advantage the internal and external information we have gathered.

The new organization in which information is effectively gathered, shared and applied has the attributes of learning organizations that Peter Senge describes in *The Fifth Discipline*. "[They are] organizations where people continually expand their capacity to create the results they truly desire, where new and expansive patterns of thinking are nurtured, where collective aspiration is set free, and where people are continually learning how to learn together."

# ENVIRONMENTAL SCANNING AND LEARNING

## Personal Benefits

One purpose of environmental scanning that we have mentioned is ensuring that the workers' knowledge in their area of specialty is current. Just as important, the scanners must use the information to challenge their personal perspectives. The personal paradigms (patterns or models) individuals bring to the activity of information scanning lead them to filter out all information that does not fit into the way they see the world. To ensure they do not reject important information, and to stretch or even replace their own paradigms, environmental scanners must be vigilant. Joel Barker, who popularized the application of the scientific concept of paradigms to the business world, said, "If something is outside of our paradigms we just don't get it." That is rather a frightening idea. How do we know when we are not getting something? Wisdom means "getting it" clearly and requires that we force ourselves to consider information to which our first reactions may be, "Crazy idea." "Wrong!" "Doesn't make sense!" It makes sense to someone. Perhaps we are the ones who are "wrong." Honestly considering information that does not fit comfortably within our usual paradigms leads us to develop new paradigms, or at least to increase the flexibility of our present ones. Challenging ourselves to consider information that we might normally discount helps open our perspectives.

Putting ourselves into new situations forces us to open up our visual patterns of thought. Robert Scott Root-Bernstein from Michigan State University has researched "how" science is done. He found that scientists who continue to make breakthroughs tend to change fields every five to ten years. He discovered that what he calls the Novice Effect seems to stimulate people. Our new mode of working with the expectation of several careers is bringing Root-Bernstein's Novice Effect to the business world.

Another common characteristic of breakthrough scientists is that they tend to be global thinkers. Root-Bernstein writes that, "They look at the world as a whole; they want to understand the whole world; they believe that there are principles that nature uses everywhere." These people demonstrate the need for an understanding of, and a belief in, a systems view of the world as well as knowledge about that world.

## SPECIALIST VS. GENERALIST

It might be expected that, in the new economy, knowledge workers would focus on gathering information and learning within their own field of specialty. But as part of the system, we must be able to understand the whole of the organization. People will continue to increase their cross-functional activities looking for opportunities to contribute to other parts of the organization and to learn from them. In environmental scanning,the broader one's knowledge base, the easier it is to identify pieces of information that will have meaning to the organization.

We have established that breakthrough ideas most often come from the novice rather than the long-term expert. Knowledge workers in the new organization must be specialists. The challenge, then, is to make sure that they are specialists with fringe perspectives. They need general eclectic knowledge and an ability to objectively monitor their own filter systems as they deal with that information.

# INFORMATION AND INNOVATION

Countless stories are told of people who were at the fringe or even outside of an industry who were responsible for major breakthroughs. People on the outside are not limited by old patterns of thinking and established assumptions and so can more easily see a new way of doing things. Outsiders can more easily be innovative. They are not hampered by professional or group paradigms and so are not pressured by peers to conform. They can afford to take the risk of coming up with a seemingly crazy idea because they do not have the worry of losing credibility with their peers.

Outsiders are also unhampered by such organizational constraints as deadlines, budgets, power and rigid structure. For example, working to organizational requirements rather than for the joy of the intellectual pursuit has been cited as an inhibitor of scientific innovation in laboratory research.

Wisdom, then, requires gathering the right information and turning it into powerful knowledge. Seeing innovative possibilities is easier for the outsider, but turning the idea into innovation is easier for the insider. How, then, as insiders, do we incorporate an outsider's perspective into our information scanning processes?

### Developing an Outsider's Perspective

Developing an outsider's perspective requires: (1) freedom to take risks; (2) the ability to set aside personal assumptions about what will work and what won't, at least temporarily; and (3) time to reflect playfully on ideas.

Achieving these requirements means a major personality change for many organizations, but it doesn't have to be a long or difficult make-over. Simple behaviors consistently practiced can bring about a speedy and substantial increase in the ability to look at information objectively and innovatively. These behaviors include making a conscious effort to encourage horizontal thinking, listening openly to unconventional ideas, challenging people's thinking, allowing people the opportunity to try out seemingly crazy ideas and treating failure as a learning experience.

The basic requirements for behavioral change apply:

• Clear expectations of the new behaviors;
• Modeling of the behaviors by the leaders;
• Recognition and reinforcement when new behaviors are displayed.

For these ideas to work, the vertical/horizontal balance must be maintained. On the horizontal side, the behaviors described above; on the vertical side, an assessment of risk impact before seemingly outlandish ideas are tried. The lower the risk, obviously, the easier it is to give the idea a try. However, there are times when even big risks are worth it, even necessary. This is when intuition comes into play.

New attitudes and behaviors will increase the effectiveness with which new information is used. New technology will allow easy access to as much data as anyone wants, and more. The key will be determining precisely what one needs and how to turn the data into information that can be used.

Organizations need to ask these questions: What kind of information do we need? How do we access information, not just data? How do we ensure that the right people have the required information? How do we ensure the information gets turned into knowledge (is used)?

A few organizations deal seriously with these questions, including Royal Dutch/Shell. Most organizations have not yet begun to consider the issue of timely and useful information, and it is unlikely that most will be able to fulfill this need entirely by themselves.

The critical need for useful information is spawning a whole new line of business within the information industry. Companies and often independent information consultants offer information-gathering services. They collect and disperse information according to specific industry or company needs. Consultants may work with a company to determine exactly what type of information is required and then devise methods for collecting and interpreting the appropriate data to create the information. The role of the internal information consultant will become standard within companies, but most will still need help from outside sources.

A leader in both timing and the degree to which its concepts are in tune with the new economy is Global Business Network. It brings people together from many different fields to help companies gain insight into the future. Clients become members of the network, which means not just receiving information but participating. GBN creates, scans and filters information with an eye to the future and forwards selected valuable pieces to clients. Providing filtered information is a valuable service, but GBN's partners recognized that the key to success in the new economy is inter-connectedness and created an even more powerful service. GBN facilitates learning conferences both in-person and on-line at which members exchange information, experience and ideas and even make connections that can lead to new relationships.

The president of the company, Peter Schwartz, emphasizes that "In an economy where knowledge and information directly improve the bottom line, personal relationships become much more important. They are the source not just of facts, but of judgment." We need others' judgments, par-ticularly those we don't immediately agree with, to continue to challenge our personal filters.

The next challenge for organizations is to develop the information value. They must understand what information they need (what questions need to be answered), how they can best gather it and how information is translated into knowledge.

As we become settled into the new economy, knowledge will increas-ingly have an economic value attached to it. The information held by an organization and the intuition with which it is applied will determine the value of a company's knowledge.

## THEORY IN ACTION

Enterprise Systems Inc. is a company that values information and its appli-cation. The company is dedicated to helping health-care organizations redesign the way they deliver care through the use of innovative software and new technology. ESI's associates are equally committed to changing the way business is done.

Enterprise Systems is one of the few companies that have lived up to the paperless-office promise. Its database system has replaced the office filing cab-inet. Associates can find any information they might need in their day-to-day activities. Information they access might include client correspondence, busi-ness-contact information and information on product and support issues.

Communicating electronically with the most up-to-date tools is a norm. As early as 1990, Enterprise Systems had an e-mail package in place that linked people who worked on site with associates on the road. In addition, e-mail was included as part of clients' systems packages, greatly enhancing ESI's communication with them. Clients readily shared highly valuable information that ESI would have been unlikely to receive otherwise.

Equally forward thinking is the company's attitude to the sharing of internal information. ESI knows that access to information is a competitive advantage. Company president Joe Carey emphasizes the importance of having "no sacred territories or grounds."

The company recognizes that associates cannot feel a sense of ownership and commitment if they are not fully informed. CEO Glenn Tullman puts out a message twice a month on strategic direction, organizational issues or information concerning clients. Quarterly meetings give associates an opportunity to share information, learn about new products and showcase what they are doing. Anyone missing meetings can get a recap on videotape and on e-mail.

Information has value only when it is used. Wise application requires an up-to-date personal knowledge base and the power to act. Enterprise Systems expects continuous learning of each associate. Carey believes that "In order for work to be rewarding, you must be learning constantly." Associates are also expected to be self-directed, to "just do it." Everyone is guided by the corporate belief that the client's needs are of paramount importance and is trusted to act with the client's interest at heart.

Associates have the knowledge that allows them to develop strong relationships with clients, understand their business needs and deliver products and services to meet these objectives. The results? Enterprise Systems has enjoyed a 98 percent client-retention rate and a growth rate of over 30 percent.

Enterprise Systems is a young, high-tech, mid-sized company. Many companies do not match its profile but its success factors are transferable.

- Open access to information ⎱ Both require trust
- A self-directed environment ⎰
- Information sharing (a priority)
- Technology that allows easy access to information and encourages communication
- Continuous learning as an expectation

## REFLECTION & APPLICATION

1. Is information valued in your organization?
• Do members of your organization see information gathering as part of their job?
• Have the organization and members determined what information is vital to their future success?

2. Do you value information?
• Do you spend some time each day scanning information in newspapers, magazines or on the Internet?
• Do you gather eclectic information, that is, do you peruse information not in your area of specialty or of immediate interest?

3. One common denominator of people who do breakthrough work is that they have broad interests and hobbies and are curious about most things.
• When you come across information with which you do not immediately agree, do you use it to challenge your thinking?
• Do you use new information to change the way you do things?

4. Here is one way to challenge traditional thinking:
• Invite outsiders to problem-solving sessions. Ensure they have different professional or functional backgrounds from yours. Our tendency is to select people who are as much like us as possible, in spite of different backgrounds. Avoid the temptation of selecting people who "think like us." The further they are from being "like us," the greater the possibility that they will see something you have missed. Though you may be impatient for a solution, the challenge will be to spend some time supplying outsiders with information, making an effort to ensure they get pure information, not already slanted by your perspective, and refraining from "that won't work" responses.
    Try this idea when you are facing a tough problem or need a particularly innovative solution.

# 6

# INTUITION

A gut feeling, a sixth sense, a hunch, knowing "it just feels right" have been experienced by everyone at some time. Wisdom results when the intuitive sense positively influences our response to information.

Leaders have always recognized the need for more than their rational abilities to cope with leadership challenges. Julius Caesar turned to soothsayers, J. P. Morgan and Mackenzie King were counseled by psychics and Ronald Reagan is said to have received advice from an astrologer.

Although most leaders do not consult psychics — or do not share that information if they do — they recognize that many, if not all, of their best decisions were not based solely on reason; they had a strong intuitive component.

*The dilemma of any statesman is that he can never be certain about the probable course of events. In reaching a decision, he must inevitably act on the basis of an intuition that is inherently unprovable. If he insists on certainty, he runs the danger of becoming a prisoner of events.*

Henry Kissinger
Quoted by Nikola Phillips,
*From Vision to Beyond Teamwork*

Successful people are often described as having a "business sense" or a "great sense of timing."

Some believe that intuition is an extra sense that is spontaneous and unpredictable. The new organization will prove these people wrong by learning to cultivate it. Strengthening intuitive powers has taken on increasing importance in the new organization for two reasons. People must function in ambiguity, in situations where there is insufficient information and where the information changes minute by minute. In addition, many people have only limited access to their intuitive powers. They have allowed their intuition to be stifled by the expectations of the traditional organization, which rewarded logic. This difficulty is compounded by the constant sensory arsenal of the modern world that makes it difficult for intuitive voices to get our attention.

John Mihalasky, who has studied executive intuition, recognized that with too much data the conscious mind interferes with the subconscious. Even if you get a "flash," the rational system is likely to destroy the intuitive component. In the new organization, data overload is inevitable. With a decrease in intuitive power, we are put in the position of having to lead and work in uncertainty and ambiguity. The irony is that this kind of situation calls for greater intuition than ever before.

We can all identify times when we have acted on an intuitive feeling and have been rewarded with successful outcomes. On the other hand, we may have had hunches that did not work, although the successes are remembered and retold. Intuitive success stories become classics.

Bill Gates recognized as a teenager that there would be a personal computer industry and that not only would it be huge, economically, but it would be a major influence on society. He and his friend, Paul Allen, "knew" when they saw the first mini-computer on the cover of *Popular Electronics* in 1975 that the new world had arrived. The "knowing" was so strong that, as Bill Gates describes the experience, ". . . panic set in. Oh no! It's happening without us!" and the two began the "two-man, shoe-string operation" that would become Microsoft, with six billion dollars a year in sales.

Roy Rowan describes how Ray Krock "discovered" McDonald's in 1952 when he was selling milkshake mixers. Krock was curious when one restaurant owned by the McDonald brothers ordered eight milkshake mixers, and he decided he had to fly to California to deliver them himself (intuition). People were lined up for the McDonalds' hamburgers. During the next five years, he franchised 228 McDonald's outlets, but he was making little. In 1960 he offered to buy the McDonald brothers out. They quoted him $2.7 million. His lawyer told him not to agree and that $2.7 million was out of his league, financially. "But," he said, "my funny-bone instinct kept urging me on." His funny-bone instinct led to today's 8,000 golden arches.

The faster the pace of change, the greater the need for intuition. Much decision making is done in pea-soup fog, which reveals only some of the information, and what is clear may not be relevant by the time decisions are implemented.

Ron Schultz discusses this dilemma in his book *Unconventional Wisdom*, and presents the following quote from Lee Iacocca: "You never get all of the facts," Iacocca says. "If you wait, by the time you do get them, your facts will be out of date because the market has moved on. . . . At some point, you have to take a leap of faith . . . because even the right decision is wrong if it is made too late."

Regis McKenna, one of North America's first and leading high-tech marketing consultants, and the man credited with creating the image of the Silicon Valley, concurs: "A decision is process. People are successful in today's high-tech world by constantly altering and adjusting to the environment. It is a constant process of change. You can't make decisions that are absolute because there is no absolute. There are only relative situations."

Adjusting to the environment requires an intuitive sense of how it is changing. It requires seeing the whole picture as a system and recognizing how one small change will impact the entire system.

The good intuition of many corporate leaders never gets turned into wisdom. It may be blocked by more senior members of management who are less intuitive or have a lower tolerance for risk. Many corporate opportunities are lost by the individual who decides to ignore the nagging voice of intuition. The risk is too high. Some risk impulses are stifled by the sense of responsibility for shareholders, and for some leaders, staff. Many more leaders' impulses are stifled by personal insecurity and a sense of needing to manage their own careers and create a favorable track record.

The result is a mediocre career. The organization that selects and rewards low-risk takers suffers the same fate. In the new economy, the mediocre will be out of the race — there is room for only winners and losers.

Studies have also validated intuition's role in corporate success. In John Mihalasky's studies, conducted over a 10-year period, executives were tested for their precognitive ability. Close to 100 percent of those who had at least doubled their company profits over the preceding five years had above-average precognitive scores. Those who had not doubled profits all scored lower than average.

## EVERYDAY INTUITION

Although hunches about hot ideas or dramatic decisions produce the most obvious examples of intuition, it is day-to-day intuition that creates the culture and generates the energy that fuels the organization. It is intuition that tells leaders to let go and hand decision-making power — traditionally theirs — to a member with a great deal less experience. It is intuition that tells the salesperson to call on someone who may not logically fit into the target market. It is intuition that tells a team member to meet with another for coffee — to find out if that individual has a concern that could impact team performance.

As organizations evolve in the new economy, there is a strong likelihood of creating conditions nonconducive to intuition. The deluge of information and data, the pace of the need for instant decisions, pressure to succeed in highly competitive environments, personally and corporately, the multitude of variables and options, and the pace of change and sense of being constantly in a catch-up or keep-up mode increase the danger that interactive signals will not even be heard, and if they are, will be ignored.

## OPENING THE INTUITIVE CHANNEL

Intuition is blocked by stress, fear and uncertainty. The command and control of traditional organizations sometimes inadvertently and sometimes intentionally intimidates individuals.

My first foray into organizational life was a summer job with an employment agency while I was still at school. I was to interview applicants, select the winners, match them to job openings with our clients.

The experience was a brief one and the only detail I remember clearly was the reason I was there such a short time — my chair. The interviewer's chair seemed to be the focal point of the organization and was highly symbolic of the entire culture. The only training I recall receiving revolved around that chair. Each work station was supplied with two chairs and it was of paramount importance that the interviewer be seated in the "right" chair. This chair was several inches higher than that of the interviewee. Interviewers were trained to position themselves carefully so that they would be looking down on (literally and figuratively) applicants, who in turn would have to look up at the interviewer.

The rationale behind intimidating individuals whose qualities we were supposed to be uncovering in order to "sell" them to the client completely eluded me. Not surprising, the same philosophy was demonstrated with equal precision in the management style. I was struck by the number of staff, depressed and several of them ill, who were trapped or had allowed themselves to be trapped in that sick organization.

So exaggerated, it was a caricature of the top-down, command-and-control organization. Whether or not by intent, all traditional structures intimidate to some extent. In some cases they result in actual fear; in others they result in caution that, although not as stressful, still stifles intuition and its transformation into wisdom.

When one is functioning in a survival mode, the focus is to keep one's head down and to take the low-risk road, which is inevitably the one paved with facts and figures.

Too many organizations are still struggling with the most basic requirements for corporate health: an environment in which people are appreciated as individuals, are recognized for strengths and where trust allows honesty, openness and risk taking. When people can relax and be themselves instead of having to calculate all of their moves, they are likely to tune in to their intuition.

John Mihalasky has labeled one intuition inhibitor the dominance factor. Whoever controls the group can impede the intuition of other members. He observed that an intuitive decision maker would have a low score in precognitive tests if she or he were controlled by someone else.

In *Knowledge and Value*, Solveig Wilkstrom and Richard Normanson discuss the need for security in developing new knowledge. "An element of uncertainty will always accompany the generation and application of new knowledge. But when the climate is one of psychological security and allows an understanding of failure, then the conditions are good for risk taking and the generation of knowledge."

# SELF-DIRECTION

When teams and individuals are effectively self-directed, the values of respect and trust are expressed to their fullest. Self-direction will have to be seen not only as a good idea, but as a fact of life as corporations become populated with knowledge workers who, by the nature of their work and their degree of specialty, will work increasingly independently.

In a self-directed environment, individuals have freedom within their parameters of authority. They are responsible and accountable for everything within those boundaries. The freedom and sense of accomplishment in a legitimate, self-directed environment is highly conducive to tapping intuition. By "legitimate" I mean that its practices match the structure, labels and rhetoric.

An airline that was making an effort to increase self-direction and ownership found that many front-line people who were ready and able were discouraged by some managers who were slower to change. Members of one team that had been empowered decided to upgrade a passenger who had a cast on her leg. There were open seats in first class and the extra legroom would mean a more comfortable flight for the customer. They were feeling wonderful about having given a customer extra service, and having done it of their own initiative, only "to have our fingers rapped," as they said, for having done it without getting approval.

In a legitimate self-directed organization, the parameters of authority are clear and people use their own judgment within the parameters. Members are expected to listen to their intuition and to apply it to make improvements and to capitalize on new opportunities.

Effective self-direction creates energy and excitement. There is a joy in performance that puts people in flow with their work. Athletes often describe moments when they are one with their game — a Wayne Gretzky who knows where the puck will be and moves there to meet it. In teamwork it becomes a synergistic experience, in which the whole is greater than the sum of its parts. Working as a synergistic team means working naturally. Working naturally with ease and joy puts people in tune with their intuition. In most organizations, unfortunately, this type of teamwork is still rare.

In the early 1990s, when most corporations were still trying to figure out how self-directed teams could best be structured and were questioning whether they could really work, one corner of IBM was doing some remarkable things. The director of the area had courageously charged the front-line staff with the job of redesigning the department around self-directed teams. A seed team put together the design and selected the leaders. The result was a completely new world of work and an organization chart that had absolutely no resemblance to the old one. There were three leaders supporting several teams each instead of one manager for every team. New practices depended on new mindsets. Leaders had to be able to let go, and team members had to be ready and able to accept new and additional responsibilities and the accountability that went with them.

Some time after the teams were up and running, I was invited to speak at a mini-conference. One of the other speakers had been a member of the seed team and was now a member of a new self-directed team. He described the new structure, its rationale and how it had come about. What struck me most were his tone and language. He described the "new" IBMers as happy campers, not as the stereotypical navy blue suited, high-powered business people who were most commonly linked to IBM. These people were working extremely hard but having fun. They even thought about work at home, not because they had to, he told the group, but because they were so enthusiastic about what they were doing. In fact, they couldn't wait to get to work to share their new ideas with other team members and to try them out.

He also talked about what had motivated them to do things very differently. It hadn't been, and still wasn't, easy. What they were doing was very different from the rest of the organization at that time. They were pioneers, and some people around them were not comfortable with the new direction and were waiting for them to fail. They had rocked the boat. They had to be highly motivated, he said, to carry on. They were motivated by a commitment to the organization, which they knew had to work differently in order to remain competitive. They were also motivated by two other factors: a desire to make their idea (the new team design) work, and a desire to enrich their personal lives, both of which were intrinsically tied to IBM's success.

Here was an environment that was both relaxed (people were at ease) and stimulating, as well as one with no boxes (manager/worker, my job/your job, home/work). Energy flowed freely and intuition was tapped. The IBM team saw each other as people with personal as well as corporate motivation and their own role at IBM as an integral part of their whole life, not an eight-hour compartmentalized component of it. The traditional organization has tried to artificially compartmentalize everything, including work and non-work lives. This unnatural state of existence creates a stressful environment that blocks energy and dulls intuition. Stress-management specialists often emphasize leaving your work at the workplace. Mentally put it in a drawer, they suggest, and lock it away until the morning. If work is joyful, this is unnecessary.

Hans Selye, the father of stress management, insisted that work is an essential part of healthy life. Long hours of work, he emphasized, do not create negative stress, as long as there is joy in the work. We can allow work to create distress or can use it to create eustress (positive stress) that personally energizes and puts us in closer touch with our intuitive natures.

## TAPPING INTUITION FOR BUSINESS WISDOM

Paradoxically, we must make a rational effort to tap nonrational intuition. Intuition can be seen in different ways. A precognitive or ESP type of experience that produces a knowing about a loved one in need, or the right numbers to pick in the lottery, is described as intuition. Occasionally business wisdom arises from this type of intuition. Often it is the result of the unconscious taking a bird's-eye view of information that has been accumulated consciously and unconsciously, both recently and over a lifetime, including the interconnections, the variables and the ramifications, and then distilling all of this into a nugget of an idea or the solution — eureka!

Roy Rowan, author of *The Intuitive Manager,* puts it this way: "It [intuition] concerns relationships, involves simultaneous perception of a whole system, and can draw a conclusion not necessarily correct without preceding through logical intermediary steps."

Henry Mintzberg describes four stages of problem solving. These can also be considered the stages for creating wisdom. They include the requirements for sparking intuition and then logically verifying intuition. Once again, therefore, we have returned to the importance of balance between process focus and task focus. The steps include:

1. Preparation (task);
2. Incubation (process);
3. Illumination (process);
4. Verification (task and process).

## Preparation

Preparation can be an immersion in the information at hand. It can include research, reading and intense analytical thinking about the current issue or problem. However, preparation can also include lifelong or career-long development of knowledge. How well we gather, interpret and assimilate information will determine the contribution we are able to make in the new organization.

## Incubation

How-to's on developing intuitive power often suggest the process begins with an intense period of conscious analysis of information followed by a complete setting aside of all conscious thoughts about it. The unconscious is then set free to do its job. The "eureka!" that emerges may happen spontaneously on the golf course when there appears to be no obvious trigger. Other flashes occur when relaxing, but in an environment with a trigger that connects and completes the work the unconscious has already done. The classic example is Archimedes' revelations about displacement that were triggered by his overflowing bath. In this case, however, the story suggests that he had not completely set the problem aside but was comfortably reflecting on it.

Reflection is not generally highly rated or rewarded in the traditional organization. This is unfortunate because a few moments of staring into space on a regular basis can lengthen the organization's shelf life.

Mintzberg's steps reinforce the importance of reflection. When people hear the suggestion that they need more time to reflect, the response is often "Reflect? We barely have time to act." This dilemma is real and not simple to solve. The reality is we do not have as much time as we would like and there is no sign that venturing further into the new economy will change that. The other reality is that we cannot afford to make anything less than the best decision and we have no time to rework mistakes or make up for mediocre decisions. We need as much help as we can get and we often ignore the help that is most accessible to us — our intuition.

Directed reflection occurs when the mind is instructed to ponder a specific problem and then is set free to work on it.

Open reflection involves sitting back and letting the mind choose its own direction, randomly picking its own place to light. It not uncommonly lights on an issue that has been steeping and comes up with interesting thoughts; on the other hand, it may not produce anything at all of interest. Whether or not there are direct outcomes, reflection allows the reasoning process to take a rest and generally relaxes and refreshes. People resume their tasks with more energy and often see a new approach after having turned away from an issue for a few minutes.

The need to relax the mind deeply in order to function at peak performance both mentally and physically has been accepted by most, and techniques such as meditation are commonly practiced by many. Meditation has not been recognized as an important practice in most organizations — yet.

## Illumination

For some people, illumination is a flash. For others, a nudge. For some, it might be a nagging idea that won't go away; for others, it is so loud a voice it cannot be ignored. Others benefit from training themselves to be better tuned to their intuition by becoming more aware of the physical needs that signal intuition for them. They may have a feeling in the stomach (a gut feel), a feeling in the chest or emotional elation. Recognizing the feeling, stopping and consciously asking oneself, Why am I feeling this way? can help trace the feeling back to the message the intuition is sending.

Another exercise for increasing our intuitive awareness is to simply jot down any apparently intuitive ideas that come to us throughout the day. Recording them makes us more aware of them and often does two things:
- We are more liable to listen to and use them as appropriate;
- The occurrence of intuitive insights increases.

## Verification

At this stage, it is time to use logic to weigh the intuitively produced idea against facts. In the end, however, particularly when there is never enough data and things change quickly, the verification is a check of the strength of the intuitive impulse. Is there any nagging doubt or is it a strong "Yes!"?

## TAPPING TEAM INTUITION

If intuition means tapping and synthesizing the unconscious store of information, team intuition must be incredibly valuable. We have referred to the importance of interconnectedness, that as the complexity of issues increases, the less able individuals are to solve problems independently. Even one's independent subterranean store of information, however massive, is often not enough. Proponents of metaphysics suggest that when we tap our highest intuitive powers, we can access the collective unconscious. That idea has certain appeal. Whether or not we believe we can tap a universal unconscious, we can tap the collective unconscious of a team.

Accessing team intuition requires group process; at the same time, the group process can stifle intuition. We have already discussed how too much incoming data can jam intuitive channels. In meetings, the contribution of information and ideas combined with verbal input (noise) can be very interruptive. Independent thinkers who work best on their own may be at the greatest disadvantage in a group process.

In addition, there is the danger of group-think. If the majority of members are thinking one way, the pressure to conform can prevent intuitive thinking and certainly intuitive contribution.

Decision-making processes are usually too hurried to allow the group to access its intuition. People complain that decision making takes too long. In my experience, the process is usually not long enough and if it is too long, it is because of an ineffective process. The task-oriented members of the group tend to push for early closure, shutting down dialogue and any reflection that could tap intuition. Teams that tap their collective intuition have well-structured processes and are skilled at dialoguing. (See the discussion and tips for dialoguing and for structuring an effective group process in chapter 12, "Team Learning.")

Organizations that make it into the new economy will be on a level playing field. They will each have effectively restructured, they will be accessing the latest technology, they will be humanistic, self-directed, team-based organizations and they will have superior knowledge. Any organizations that do not fit this description will have fallen by the wayside. Companies, then, will have equal opportunities and equal strengths; they will be running neck and neck. Where, then, is the edge?

The degree to which a company taps its intuitive powers and creates wisdom may be its only opportunity for differentiation.

---

# REFLECTION & APPLICATION

### I. Exercising Wisdom and Intuition

Mintzberg suggests that problems are solved in four stages.

1. Preparation
2. Incubation
3. Illumination
4. Verification

Illumination (step 3) can be activated only if steps 1 and 2 have been completed. You can encourage your own intuition and that of your team by ensuring that steps 1 and 2 are in place.

Consider your own problem-solving practices and/or those of your team.

In steps 1 and 2:

• Do you spend sufficient time examining all information?

• In team problem solving, do you dialogue in order to fully explore and understand members' ideas and points of view?

• In individual problem solving, do you look to others for their knowledge and ideas or as a sounding board for yours? ( i.e., Do you recognize your interconnectedness and access the system of which you are a part?)

• Do you spend time reflecting on issues and the information you have?

• Do you leave incubation time for important issues? Although there are crises, there are few decisions that can't be left for a day after the initial discussion.

In step 4:

• Once the solution or idea emerges, do you take time to ensure a decision will be a wise one by examining it with your reasoning faculties?

• If facts suggest weakness, do you return once more to reflection to check whether or not there is still a strong feeling that this is "right" in spite of the facts?

## II. Encouraging Reflection and Intuition

People whose intuition has paid off agree with Ray Krock's suggestion that if it is right, "that feeling" just won't go away.

Reflection and intuition can be encouraged by structured processes that introduce triggers, such as pictures or word associations. The ancient Chinese classic, the *I Ching* or *Book of Changes*, dating back to the second or third millennium B.C., is used to call upon a higher wisdom. It is a collection of 64 hexagrams; reflecting on a hexagram with a specific problem in mind is meant to set the mind on different paths that can create new insights related to the problem. The last of the 64 hexagrams reads like this:

### The Judgment
Before contemplation. Success.
But if the little fox, after nearly completing the cross,
Gets his tail in the water,
There is nothing that would further.

### The Image
Fire over water:
The image of the condition before transition
Thus the superior man is careful
In the differentiation of things,
So that each finds its place.

Alan Watts suggests that "The comment is invariably ocular; vague and ambivalent, but a person taking it seriously will use it like a Rorschach blot and project into it, from his 'unconscious,' intuitive self, whatever there is for him to find in it."

This is not a method that the Western mind, used to logical analysis to solve the problem at hand, can easily embrace. Intellectually, however, we can understand this as a trigger for reflection and more intuitive thinking. A modern variation, more compatible with the organizational mind, is presenting a group with a quotation to reflect on. The quotation may be related to the modern business world (more comfortable to the task-oriented mind) or can be from any other source from history to fairy tales. The group is asked to reflect on the quotation and to share ideas that the quotation triggers, related to the discussion at hand.

The purpose of the activity is three-fold: to trigger intuitive responses; to exercise participants' intuitive thinking processes; and to reinforce the importance of reflection and the expectation that it become a practice. Reflection will be an accepted part of the way the successful new organization works.

## III. Making Reflection an Expectation

People have learned their harried "can't stop for anything" habit and they can learn a more balanced task/process habit that includes time for reflection. Changing behavior usually needs support. Behavior is most likely to change when the need for change is evident and when there is an expectation that change will take place. The support may include:

• Casual but frequent and consistent remarks about the need to reflect;

• Modeling reflection — "I'm going to put my feet up out in the court-yard for 10 minutes and reflect on this," or "I'm going to go and have a coffee and think about this for a couple of minutes";

• Formal learning workshops on reflection.

### *Tips for Creating the Expectation of Reflection*
**One-on-One**

If you are planning to discuss something one-on-one, suggest to the other person, "Take 10 minutes and jot down some ideas and then let's get together to talk about it."

Once reflection becomes a norm, the suggestion may simply be "think about this" or "reflect on this for a few minutes before we get together on it." However, in the beginning, when reflection is a new idea, if the suggestion is simply "think about it," people will do something else that seems more pressing with that time. After all, they have been conditioned to believe that they can just "wing" a discussion. No preparation is needed.

### In Groups
*Preparing for a Meeting*

When calling a meeting to make a decision, emphasize that you want people to reflect on the topic beforehand. Give some specific directions, or it likely won't happen. For example:

1. "Come with two new ideas about . . ." or "Come with two pros and two cons, and your rationale behind them."

2. "Spend some time thinking about a subject, and then talk with three

people about it. Think about their perceptions and come prepared with some ideas."

3. Provide participants with an article to read about the subject and ask them to come with ideas that it has triggered.

*During the Meeting*

1. In the session, begin with the expectation that the preparatory reflection was given attention. Some group leaders start out with a statement that sends the wrong message, one that accepts the status quo and mediocrity (e.g., "Did anyone have time to . . ." or "Who did some thinking on . . ."). The leader must assume people have followed through and act accordingly. "Let's hear from each of you the thoughts you have developed. Please give as much detail as possible because we want to increase our understanding as well as trigger new thinking on this." Initially, some may not be prepared to fully contribute, but they will soon learn that, if the leader is consistent, reflection is expected as part of the way the group works.

2. Introduce the concept of wisdom, including intuition and reflection. Ask team members to identify practices the team can adopt that will increase reflection and tap the group's intuition. Ensure the team pauses on a regular basis to check whether the selected practices are consistently used.

3. At the beginning of a meeting, provide some time for silently generating ideas. "Jot down a couple of ideas on. . . ." If a decision needs to be made quickly within a meeting, take a 10-minute reflection break: "This is an important decision. I'd like each of you to give it a few more minutes thought. Let's spread out and be comfortable, walk around if you like, but please let's not talk so that we don't interrupt others' thinking."

Don't link this with a coffee break or time will be spent filling cups, chit-chatting and running to washrooms. Thinking, of course, can also happen while we're doing other things, but the purpose of this activity is to provide silent reflection time, which is a different thinking environment than the usual, and to create a new norm within the organization — it is okay and, in fact, expected that people take time out to think.

## IV. Recognizing that Feeling

Some people are strongly linked to their intuition and it shouts loudly when it needs their attention. (Actually, it shouts when *they* need *its* attention or help.) Many, however, who are highly task oriented, stressed or immersed in data, don't readily feel the nudging of their intuition.

Does your intuition speak clearly to you? If not, do you have recognizable and specific signs that tell you it is nudging you?

Some people call it simply a "nagging feeling" that no one can verbalize, but everyone recognizes when they experience it. Others experience physical sensations in the stomach (gut feeling) or in the chest area. Intuition both produces ideas or solutions and evaluates them. The physiological signals are communicating "go/no go," "not quite" or "think about it some more."

Once you have identified your intuition's tap on the shoulder, pay attention to the signal. When you feel it, stop and reflect. Awareness of intuition can be strengthened through exercise.

# 7

# A SENSE OF SELF

The sense of self is an important part of the intuitive process. On a conscious level, a sense of self is reflected in corporate values if they describe the way the organization actually works. On an intuitive level there is a deeper sense of self, including how the organization works, who we are, what works for us and what doesn't, what we need and what we do best (most naturally and with the greatest of ease).

Not having a sense of self or ignoring it has been a major contributing factor in many errors in strategic direction. Molson Breweries, an established Canadian company, bought Diversey Corp., an industrial cleaning business, in 1978. In 1989, Molson sold 60 percent of Molson Breweries to other brewers. After several years of increasing losses at Diversey, Molson sold it in 1996 for far less than it had hoped. It had taken a huge risk on diversification at the expense of a healthy brewing business.

When diversification fails there can be many contributing factors, from lack of market knowledge to common management *faux pas* such as poor planning. However, lack of a sense of self is often a major contributing factor when conglomerates run into problems. The expertise developed by Molson in its 209 years of making beer allows it to respond instinctively (if it chooses to listen to its intuition) in the beer industry. It did not have that intuitive judgment about the cleaning business. Presently it is moving back to its core businesses — beer and sports.

A keen sense of self is essential to making the right diversification decisions. As businesses recreate themselves — as they will be required to do to an even greater degree in the new economy — the innate sense of self will become far more pivotal but also far more elusive. What, for example, is banking today and what will it be tomorrow?

Not long ago, a bank's identity was clear. "The Bank," to most people, did not mean The Bank of Nova Scotia or Citibank, but their local branch at the corner where they went every week to cash their paycheck and perhaps put a little aside in a savings account. The manager spent the day in the office greeting customers who came looking for assistance (managers did not go knocking on doors). The customers knew the staff by name, not because they wore plastic name tags, but because the customers had been served by them for so many years.

The bank helped fulfill big dreams through home mortgages and, before credit cards, the little dreams, like having enough money set aside for Christmas gifts, by offering the Christmas Club savings account.

People saw the bank not so much as a service provider, but more as something they belonged to. The bank was part of the community; it was there to help. Everyone knew what the bank's business was — savings and loans. In corporate banking, the identity was equally clear.

In most cases today, the bank's identity is clear to neither the bank nor the customer. One of the challenges the banking industry has been facing is that the old sense of self was deeply rooted, and although banking has changed drastically, the old sense of self has not fully evolved into a new sense of self.

No industry is more traumatically affected in the transition to the new economy than the financial sector. Technology, new competitors, a myriad of new products and services, the disappearance of geographic boundaries and government deregulation mean that banks are looking for new identities. Whether banks *per se* will even exist in the twenty-first century is an open question. The consumer no longer has to depend on them to fill the traditional needs met by banks: a place to safely save and earn income on deposits and a place to borrow. For example, mutual fund companies encourage customers to use their fund as a checking account, providing check-writing privileges.

As a physical entity, the bank branch is disappearing. Already some banks are branchless. First Direct, part of Midland Bank, in the United Kingdom provides all services through phone and ATMs only. ATMs, telephone and PC banking are replacing branches. Traditional bankers are becoming "suitcase bankers" who work from home.

Moving services from branches means cost savings, but it also means a very different sense of self that everyone in the company must be in tune with if they are to respond wisely to problems, challenges and opportunities.

How do invisible staff develop relationships with invisible customers? How do you develop customer loyalty? Individual banks must have a clear sense of self and become creative in finding ways of communicating their uniqueness to the customer.

Some companies are able to maintain their present business in the new economy; others are taking what they believe to be the necessary risk of reinventing themselves. Through the reinvention process, it is very difficult to maintain a sense of self.

Wal-Mart has been a company with a very strong sense of self instilled by its founder, Sam Walton. It was the small-town "5 and Dime" with city volume discounts. No matter how many square feet a Wal-Mart actually occupied, it had a down-home friendliness about it. A sense of self was clear and showed in the pride of Wal-Mart employees. Sam Walton ensured that each employee had a strong sense of who Wal-Mart was, not only through tradition but by sharing core business information. This gave people a deeper understanding of the business and also demonstrated Sam's respect for his employees. He believed employees should be treated as partners and called them "associates" long before the term became popular. Most important, the sense of the Wal-Mart self was communicated by Sam himself: out-front, fun loving, caring, spontaneous, forward thinking and in touch with people.

Since Sam Walton's death, the retail industry has met increased challenges. David Glass, Wal-Mart's CEO, has taken the company down new paths. Wal-Mart's identity is now less certain. Some senior people who were part of Sam Walton's Wal-Mart have left. Some stores are reputed to lack the old Wal-Mart service and care of premises. One Canadian Wal-Mart store toyed with unionization. In the end it was turned down by a healthy percentage of employees, but Wal-Mart described it as a wake-up call.

Glass is focusing on food retailing. Wal-Mart traditionally provided volume discounting, usually found only in cities, to small towns in the southern and midwestern states. Now Wal-Mart stores are common in urban areas. In addition, Wal-Mart has gone international in a major way. The degree to which Wal-Mart can maintain, or perhaps reenergize, its sense of self will to a great extent determine the success with which it incorporates the myriad of changes. The new Canadian Wal-Mart, however, credits its sense of self, and its ability to communicate that identity and its values in such a way that new employees embrace them, with growth from a 22 percent market share to 40 percent in two years.

As businesses reinvent themselves, it is critical to identify whether the business is retaining the core being of its original (or previous) self. If so, it needs to be defined, talked about and celebrated. As new pieces of the new identity emerge, they too need to be clearly defined, talked about and praised. Absorbing a new sense of self requires reflection time.

People need the opportunity to ask and discuss, Who are we today? What is different from yesterday? What is the same? What does this mean as to who we are, the service or product we deliver, and how we communicate who we are? What are our new critical success factors (what are the areas in which we must achieve, if we are to succeed in our new business)? What are we particularly proud of? What do we do best?

A sense of who we are provides a sense of belonging and commitment. How can people be committed if they are not sure to what they are supposed to be committed, or whether their commitment is worthwhile? Without an instinctive sense of self, people cannot respond with wisdom.

# Part III

# INTER-
# CONNECTEDNESS

Visualize the organization not as a building or group of buildings populated by people all performing specific tasks, but as a body of knowledge. Perhaps thousands of different kinds of knowledge make up the body of knowledge that is the organization. Each member contributes to the body of knowledge. The body of knowledge creates the products or services and directs the continuous reshaping of itself, ensuring an organizational fit with the changing world.

As a collection of knowledge, these pieces of expertise can do little to fulfill the organization's mandate or potential. Only when they are connected do they become purposeful.

# 8

# THE QUANTUM ORGANIZATION

"Go take a quantum leap!" is not an insult, but a challenge to explore the new, risky and high-energy world in which everything is connected. .

The Newtonian world was one that was easy to live with and live in. Its logic and constancy offered reassurance and comfort. It was based on materialism and reductionism. In it, we focused on the pieces, not the whole, on things rather than relationships. Everything was neatly compartmentalized. Its laws of cause and effect and its logical, solid building blocks appealed to the rational mind.

Uncertain, dynamic, dualistic, interconnected. This is the world as described by the new sciences. It is a world that works through the process of quantum leaps — tiny but explosive jumps that particles of matter undergo in moving from one place to another. They are matter, then energy and then matter again.

In the quantum world, the importance of the relationship is highlighted. It is a systems world that is constantly created and recreated by the relationship between its subatomic particles.

Niels Bohr proclaimed that "Anyone who is not shocked by quantum theory has not understood it."

The man-made world mirrors our interpretation of the nature of the world we live in. Until recently, the world man constructed reflected the Newtonian world. Politically, economically, organizationally, it has been a world of compartments and building blocks, walls and separation; them and us.

The traumatic transition from the industrial-based society to the new economy has been a dramatic shift from a Newtonian to a quantum world. The tearing down of the Berlin Wall was perhaps one of the first symbolic gestures that heralded the new world. Free trade, the European Economic Union, partnerships between private and public sectors, union and management beginning to come together, the struggle of left- and right-wing parties trying to maintain a unique identity in a world of common causes. The list of examples of the tearing down of walls and decompartmentalizing could fill pages. Perhaps one of the most remarkable signals of the changing world, however, was the response to Saddam Hussein's invasion of Kuwait in 1991. This was the first time in history that countries came together to create a world army to fight a common cause.

Organizational examples are equally plentiful, such as cross-functional teams and open information sharing. People no longer work in compartments.

Perhaps the enormous change we have been experiencing is a natural major correction of a material world that had become completely incompatible with the true nature of the world. Technology has spurred the change on.

If you sat down to write that long list of examples of the Newtonian world versus the new, you would also identify some exceptions. There are a few Republican isolationists and a few hard-line unions that have not yet recognized the need to be a part of the new world and continue to fight impotently from without; there are a few management groups that have not learned how to increase their own power by empowering others. When major change is experienced, there are always those who hold on to or revert to the old, which is more comfortable and may appear more logical, at least based on the world the way it used to be. These people may slow down the transition to a totally interconnected world, but they cannot stop it.

People who are coming to understand the new organization, whether or not they relate it to quantum mechanics, see an organization that is unpredictable and constantly changing, where paradoxes and ambivalence reign and relationships overrule compartments. Focusing on the relationship or process is like looking at the photographic negative of an organization. It is focusing on what appears to be the insubstantial blank spaces between the tasks, the job descriptions, the roles and the people. This apparently blank space is where the energy and success of the organization actually lie.

How well we develop the invisible relationships will determine the health of the new Quantum Organization. These relationships will most strongly be connected when members of the organization see and respond to the organization and the world around it as a whole, a system to which they are vitally connected and are a small but influential part.

# 9

# MAKING THE
# CONNECTION

Taking the quantum leap into the new organization entails understanding that the organization and the world of which it is a part is a system, and recognizing that the power lies in the spaces between the things, in the usually invisible relationships. Each member of the organization by his or her actions continuously contributes to or diminishes the quality of the whole of which he or she is a part. This recognition is at one time empowering and burdensome.

We have for years said that "people count" and "individuals make a difference," but these were platitudes rather than beliefs. It made good sense that people should make a difference. Could they, would they, did they? Most people would have responded — "not really." Now it is not just a matter of believing that an individual's contribution is important, but it is a fact, a given in the new organization.

In the new organization, where independent knowledge workers make a strong contribution to the organization's success, contributions happen as a result of, and through, interactions.

The increased importance of interconnectedness has been intuitively recognized outside of the new organization for several years. Networking has become the way to sell products and services, to find jobs, to share ideas and support one another in career and spiritual development. Always an effective route to getting whatever it is you are after, in the past networking was seen as back-room, old-boys' stuff. Now it is the stuff of breakfast meetings, lunch meetings, dinner meetings and tête-à-tête meetings over coffee at Starbucks. Network meetings established specifically to share leads are attended by everyone from mechanics and plumbers to real estate salespeople and consultants. Direct marketing is being described as the retail wave of the future.

Why this shift from impersonal resumes, cold calls and old-fashioned retail stores? The old methods that matched the traditional vertical world where everything was compartmentalized no longer work well enough. They are out of sync with the new-systems world in which the power of connecting with others is becoming more fully realized. That power is being felt in the outcomes of these connections, be they job leads or sales. But just as important, it is felt in the charge of personal energy that people who network gain from their connection with others.

We are drawn to more personal contacts now than in the past, partly because the human need is greater. Increased work loads, constant change, the need for continuous learning and, for many, personal financial pressures at home caused by the global economic readjustments have resulted in increased levels of stress. Personal energy is being drained.

Added to this is the paradoxical nature of the new technology with which most of us spend a large portion of our time. While it is capable of connecting us with others as never before, at the same time it means we are often interacting with computers rather than people. Many years ago, John Naisbitt coined the phrase "high-tech, high-touch." The further we move into a high-tech environment, the greater our need for human interaction.

Turning to others is also an acknowledgment that one can no longer be all things to all people, or indeed even the expert, without some help. The pace of change and flood of new information mean that our own learning and experience are not enough. We must tap the learning and experience of others.

Connecting with others allows us to supplement our personal knowledge and experience, to find more creative solutions to our more complex problems, to find the contact we need for taking the next step in whatever we may be undertaking, and perhaps most important, to renew the reserve of personal energy that is so easily spent in the new world of work.

Those who are not searching out opportunities for interconnectedness are having them thrust upon them. As more organizations honestly demonstrate the belief that decisions must be made by the experts and that the experts are the people doing the job, people are being brought together to share information, solve problems and come to agreement on the solution.

Even though the concept of teams has been a focus in many organizations for some time, the importance of interconnectedness and what it entails is just beginning to be fully realized and demonstrated within organizations.

Visualize the organization not as a building or group of buildings populated by people all performing specific tasks, but as a body of knowledge. Perhaps thousands of different kinds of knowledge make up the body of knowledge that is the organization. Each member contributes to the body of knowledge. The body of knowledge creates the products or services and directs the continuous reshaping of itself, ensuring an organizational fit with the changing world.

As a collection of knowledge, these pieces of expertise can do little to fulfill the organization's mandate or potential. Only when they are connected do they become purposeful.

Once the individuals in a company are fully connected, enormous power and success will be generated. This will happen when members of the organization recognize the importance of connecting with others, have the personal skills to make the connections, become proactive in creating them and become adept at forming highly effective teams.

As always, change starts with the individual. The personal vertical/horizontal balance strongly influences one's natural tendency and ability to interconnect. Those individuals who have a strong preference for the interactive mode have always been natural networkers. They are the ones who always know what's going on, or can find out by picking up the phone. If you need to know where to go in the organization for particular help, they will inevitably know just the right person. These individuals have always understood that people are interdependent and therefore must be interconnected in order to function well. However, even those in-the-know people may be only superficially connected. They are collectors and conveyors of information. They are often not fully using these connections to share, examine and apply information in creative ways to enhance outcomes.

Others work very independently and it seldom occurs to them to pick up the phone to get information from someone else who might help them with the task at hand, to inform another person who may be affected by what they are doing, or simply to bounce ideas off someone else who may offer a different perspective. These individuals are still working vertically. To these individuals, interconnectedness does not come automatically.

In *The Flexible Organization*, Barbara Forisha-Kovach suggests that approximately 50 percent of people are task oriented by nature. The emphasis again is on finding a vertical/horizontal balance in the way individuals work. The individual who is highly task oriented, particularly if he or she has a strong independent dimension, is unlikely to initiate the connections that would benefit himself or herself and the organization. The individual who is highly process oriented will likely make the connections but may not follow through to realize any benefits.

Individual behaviors conducive to making true connections may also be limited by personal paradigms of what works and what doesn't, professional paradigms and priorities, personal or work-unit agendas, old organizational behaviors that have been well reinforced or even old organizational baggage. People may have come out of their organizational boxes but many are still trapped in professional and personal boxes. Once individuals learn to break down all walls and are effectively interconnected, they will realize their personal power. They will make a valuable contribution to their organization.

# 10

# A NEW KIND OF TEAMWORK

Knowledge teams drive the new organization. They are the most sophisticated and most powerful version of interconnectedness. When a collection of knowledge pieces optimally connect, that much-talked-about but seldom-experienced synergy results. When this high-powered interconnectedness becomes the norm, success is the outcome.

Knowledge teams can take any form, from a work unit, a management group, a task force, a project team to any other group that comes together to achieve a common goal. Team members may meet together face to face regularly or may be miles apart and meet only electronically. They may be a permanent team (although permanent is perhaps an anachronism today) or have a very short life span.

## EFFECTIVE TEAMS

In the traditional organization of the industrial-based economy, and in many organizations today, teams are mandated by the organization (e.g., a self-directed, work-unit team or project team) or result from an organizational initiative (e.g., reengineering teams or quality-improvement teams). In the new organization, teams emerge more spontaneously as members recognize and act on opportunities to create superior outcomes by connecting with others. Teams that come together quickly on their own initiative for a specific need and disperse quickly will become more common and more crucial. In other words, teamwork takes place in the new organization with varying degrees of formality.

## Spontaneous Teams

Spontaneous teamwork happens when someone sticks his or her head into someone else's work space and asks, "Have you got a minute? I want to bounce something off you," and an energetic, casual, but purposeful dialogue ensues. Others may join in and new ideas are generated that lead to outcomes that would not have been produced otherwise. There is a serendipitous quality to this type of teamwork. Although casual and unplanned, it is productive. It is not just a positive interaction but one that makes a difference.

David Hurst refers to these informal interactions as bubbles. "A bubble is a minimalist organization: there is a transparent boundary that separates the inside from the outside, and that's it. Bubbles are temporary, transparent, soft, almost playful structures that cluster together to form easy alliances with each other."

Perhaps the most important words in his description are "playful" and "easy." These are not stressful, forced interactions in which members warily watch one another for hidden agendas. Neither are they a chore. The encounters are relaxed, natural, energetic, with an element of joy.

On one hand, this is the most basic form of teamwork; on the other, paradoxically, it is the most sophisticated. Working without structure appears deceptively easy. This kind of productive spontaneity can happen only when the levels of trust are high. To get to this point, the organization must develop a culture of openness in which individuals feel good about themselves. It also requires well-honed group-process skills, developed so well in more formal team processes that they are easily applied in these informal sessions with no conscious thought.

A warning note. Several people in a work unit of a company in the financial industry believed they were experiencing this type of spontaneous teamwork. A closer look at interactions in the unit revealed that a few people who got along well together and spent a great deal of time together over coffee and lunch were naturally exchanging ideas. Decisions frequently flowed from these exchanges. However, others who had important perspectives to contribute to the discussion were excluded. These people felt, and in fact were, disempowered and at the fringe. Because valuable information was overlooked in the informal discussions, the quality of the outcomes was questioned. These interactions were spontaneous but did not produce effective outcomes.

Spontaneous teamwork requires that anyone with something to contribute be welcome to join the informal process and that the right people ultimately have input. This does not mean that these informal processes happen only when the right people are available. That obviously would negate the most important element of spontaneity. It means that team members are always cognizant of other members' potential contribution and/or need to be informed, and ensure everyone is included or updated as appropriate. The frequency and quality of spontaneous teamwork is a barometer of the organization's level of development.

In describing organizations compatible with the industrial-based economy versus those compatible with the information-age economy, we described people in the old world working in boxes and people in the new world working as a system. When spontaneous teamwork is the norm, people are working effectively as a system.

## Need-Driven Teams

Need-driven teams use more formal processes than those of spontaneous teamwork. They are initiated and driven by team members. These processes do not result from a management mandate, organizational structure or a formal program, such as reengineering, which dictates the necessity. These interactions take place in a formal meeting setting. They occur when members are sufficiently outward looking to recognize an opportunity to enhance an outcome through teamwork and take the initiative to make it happen.

These teams are usually short lived. They may exist for one meeting or several. They are usually tactical by nature, quickly formed and quickly disbanded once the purpose is fulfilled. They are often, but not necessarily, cross functional and are becoming more common as organizations continue to encourage self-direction. In addition, finding ways to communicate the expectation that people look for opportunities to connect outside of their immediate work team, such as Sun Life's emphasis on neighborhood teams, is important in instilling the new behavior.

Like spontaneous teamwork, need-driven teams will form when members are outward looking, understand the importance of interconnectedness and work in a permeable organization where openness is the norm.

## Mandated Teams

Mandated teams form an eclectic group with one thing in common: they are required by the organization. Included here are work-unit teams, both traditional (reporting to a manager or supervisor, possibly called a leader) and self-directed, management teams, task forces, project teams, quality-improvement teams, reengineering teams and so on.

Mandated teams will continue to form the foundation of the new organization. There will be far fewer traditional teams and more highly focused teams with shorter average life spans than in the past and made up of self-directed knowledge workers.

## Virtual Teams

Virtual teams seldom have the opportunity to come together around a table to develop plans or make decisions. Members may be working from home offices or from a laptop work station in their car, from across the country or from the other side of the world. The new organization must be able to attract and tap the best expertise wherever it may be located. A team may be made up of knowledge workers based around the globe. The result is not only the virtual team, but in many ways a virtual organization. New technology makes it easy to connect, but creating a high performance invisible team is not as easy.

Virtual teams require that particular issues be carefully addressed.

• How do you manage people you cannot see?

• How can people who seldom or never see one another interact effectively enough to qualify as a team?

• How do you ensure that people who are members of a virtual team are pulling in the same direction?

### Managing the Invisible

Self-direction is essential; in fact, it is the only management option in the new organization. Organizations that have already begun to manage this way have a huge head start over those who have not.

In virtual teams, there is a component of individual self-management and one of team self-management. Both are dependent on clear parameters provided by the organization. Self-management requires structure and clarity:

1. Clear definition of purpose and mandate;
2. Parameters of authority;
   - Decisions that are within the power of the team (negotiated with the organization/management);
   - Decisions that are within the power of the individual (agreed upon within the team).

### Accountability

Individual performance and outcomes must be very specifically tied to individual interests if the level of accountability required in a self-directed virtual team is to be achieved.

- Performance outcomes must be defined and contracted.
- Performance indicators (the markers along the way) must be defined and used as measurements.
- The "So what's?" must be defined. What if outcomes are not achieved? Are outcomes tied to income either through salary increases or more likely bonuses or profit sharing? Do outcomes determine whether or not the members and/or the team gets a chance to play another round?

Individuals working in a team must be accountable for not only their personal performance but team performance. Ideally, individual members' performance is based on:

- Individual performance and contributions including knowledge, skills, application of both and outcomes created;
- The team's performance measured against contracted outcomes;
- The individual's contribution to the team as evaluated by other team members, including his or her skills and knowledge contributions to the team, plus teamwork contributions, for example, sharing of the load and sharing information.

### Creating a Sense of Team Cohesiveness With Invisible Partners

Technology is the virtual team's enabler. The virtual team's access to technology, however, is no greater an assurance of success than is the traditional team's access to a meeting room. How well the team manages its process is the key determinant of its success. The team manages the process by a set of team agreements that establishes how the team will work.

The quality of the team agreements, along with the clarity of purpose and roles and responsibilities, will determine the degree of cohesiveness of the group and ultimately its success. For virtual teams these should include agreements on: what the team can do to compensate for the lack of physical proximity; when and how team members will communicate; the team's critical success factors (the areas in which it must excel if it is to be successful); priority activities; electronic meeting procedures; expected behaviors, for example, that everyone make electronic meetings a priority and that members share information openly.

As the team evolves, the required behavioral agreements will become more evident. These agreements are in place to shore up any weak spots in the team; although some working agreements should be put in place as soon as the team is formed, the list should not be written in stone. Agreements must periodically be reviewed, agreements massaged, new ones added, or perhaps those that have become a norm or habit deleted.

To be useful, agreements must be used. It must be clear to team members that agreements entail a commitment, and that members will hold one another to them. On a regular basis the team must check how members are doing. Are they living up to their agreements? If not, do they have the right agreements? What do they need to do differently?

Like all teams, the virtual team must vigilantly manage this process: if it does not, it will suffer. The difference is, its performance will suffer more quickly and perhaps to a greater degree. A dysfunctional process is even more difficult to fix when people cannot meet in person or connect spontaneously.

Technology makes virtual teams possible. However, teams that work best still come together periodically face to face or at least, initially, for an orientation, focusing and team-development session. Coming together accelerates the development of relationships and understanding, results in stronger support for the team agreements, and generates an energy and enthusiasm that cannot be developed electronically.

# THEORY IN ACTION

A virtual team of even four or five people faces special challenges. Imagine a team of 700! The IBM software-development team building the VisualAge for C$^{++}$ $^{TM}$ product consists of some 700 people located at five sites across North America.

The team faces many challenges, some inherent to the industry, some tied to the nature of a virtual team and some to the cultural changes taking place at IBM. The perspectives in the remainder of this section were provided by Peter Beggs, a team member based in Toronto, with input from other team members. The challenges he describes and the strategies for meeting them can be applied to most types of teams. They are particularly important to virtual teams.

## The Challenges

### Effectiveness in a Highly Demanding Industry

*VisualAge* is an advanced visual-application development tool suite for application programmers. This product competes in the highly competitive and very volatile software marketplace. Technology becomes "hot" almost overnight, and quick delivery is of paramount importance. Furthermore, as the software industry matures, products are becoming increasingly complex, and customers are more sophisticated and demanding.

### Commitment

We need commitment both to the project and to ourselves as an organization. When an individual or small team can be successful in their own right, whether or not the larger team is successful, gaining commitment to the overall goal can be difficult.

Commitment can also be affected by lack of trust between teams, between teams and leaders and by confusion. Confusion can be created, for example, by the lack of an agreed-upon process or our inability to follow a prescribed process.

Ironically, individual pursuits of excellence can also result in lack of buy-in. To explain, these 700 people are all professionals, well educated and knowledgeable in their field of expertise. They will argue strongly if they disagree with a priority or decision. Without strong leadership, clear definition of roles and process, individuals will not buy into a decision and may pursue another tack because they firmly believe they are right. This kind of challenge is often presented by knowledge workers.

### Accountability

We continue to work to manage the accountability challenge. Unfortunately, we have had instances when a product failed to ship because of a problem for which no one accepts ownership. Teams may have delivered what they specifically committed and point to inadequacies in other teams as being the source of the problem.

## Working on the Solutions

### Vision

We need to know where we are going. Everyone needs to be able to articulate the vision and answer key questions. Who is the customer? What problems are we trying to solve? When must we ship? Do we understand the competition?

The vision can be rendered useless if endlessly debated. It results in what we call "churn," turmoil with no forward movement.

The vision needs to be written simply, clearly and briefly. It must be constantly repeated to ensure the message is remembered consistently and is always in front of people. Because the industry is changing so quickly, we are learning that the vision should be executed in small steps over short periods of time, such as six to nine months. An entire team should not be required to deliver any one step to avoid the entire team being held up if a problem occurs. We need to be organized as a team of smaller teams, each acting on a piece of the vision. We must avoid overcomplicating each step or, in IBM terms, "boiling the ocean."

### Organization and Structure

To help increase accountability, improve communication, reduce the churn and build the team as a cohesive group, a new organizational structure has been put in place. A Business Council that charters development leads application development. The Business Council contracts with a Product Team to deliver a new product. The Product Team is made up of all the groups necessary to deliver the product, including Product Development, Service, Finance, Marketing and Vendoring.

The contract includes what will be delivered, when and at what cost.

A contract is also drawn up between the Product Team and a third team, the Release Team, which has representatives from each technology that is being delivered in the product. Detailed contracts sharpen focus, clarify expectations and define accountability.

The contract is still evolving. Issues being explored are the level of detail required and the nature of the penalty clause, should agreements not be met.

## Changing the Culture

IBM is a highly successful company whose traits have become folklore — the blue suits, the steadfast, mature and high-performance work force. The policy, process and expectations that built IBM are slow to change.

At one time IBM had virtually no external competition. The assumption of the greater IBM success meant divisions concentrated on their own success and the divisions competed among themselves. Focusing on the smaller personal picture rather than on the larger IBM was encouraged by the measurement and evaluation systems, which emphasized the success of the individual, subproject and site.

Now individuals are being challenged to take responsibility for the greater IBM. Long-term habits and mindsets are not easy to change. The crossover to the new culture will be completed with the help of leadership, human-resource policy change, the retirement of some who cannot make the adjustments and the courage of grass-roots efforts.

The following are some of the difficult areas of change that IBM is working on:

- *Moving from a strongly defined management hierarchy to a team of leaders. The president, Lou Gerstner, expects everyone to be a leader.*

The characteristics of a good leader, as described by Gerstner, include:

| | |
|---|---|
| Customer insight | Decisiveness |
| Break-set thinking | Organizational capability |
| Drive to achieve | The ability to develop talent |
| Team leadership skills | Personal dedication |
| Straight talk | Passion for the business |
| Team work | |

- *Seeing oneself as a leader to ensure commitment and increased accountability.*

• *Basing an individual's evaluation and subsequent merit pay on the success of the company and product rather than individual contribution.*

Performance evaluations have been redesigned to emphasize the importance of both teamwork and personal accountability. Personal evaluations are called Personal Business Commitments and contain three sections: the Commitment to Win, the Commitment to Execute and the Commitment to the Team. Peer input is part of the evaluation.

• *Defining success as having a well-honed skill-set versus promotion alone.*

The next step will be the simplification of the system of job levels by broadening job bands. There will be fewer categories with more opportunity for learning, skill development and movement within each category. This is meant to encourage people to build skill rather than simply work for promotions.

• *Putting greater value on building skill-sets for the future rather than guaranteed employment.*

There is significant emphasis now on individual skills and organizational development. Guaranteed employment is no longer a practice and employees must earn their keep. Each of us must build skills to ensure we are employable. We develop resumes as an indicator of that employability.

Each of these is changing the IBM culture to one of increased self-direction, responsibility for self, and accountability for the success of the company and its products. All teams will work with greater ease once the cultural shift is completed. Large virtual teams, particularly, will experience the benefits.

## Communication

In a small on-site team, communication is much easier. A small team can gather at any time in one room. Even if the vision of the group is not written, priorities and concerns are better known. As the group becomes very large and virtual, priorities, decisions and even the vision itself can be interpreted differently, and people can easily become disgruntled because they do not know what's going on. At times of churn — when major decisions are being made — unless there is high quality communication that keeps everyone in the loop, the team as a whole loses its synergy and cohesiveness.

General mechanisms for communication include electronic forums, online libraries, team publications as well as specific project documentation. Writing things down, including decisions, has a unique way of highlighting problems and accelerating decisions. Of course, people need to read the information, so it must be issued with care so as not to produce overload.

Electronic mail is pervasive at IBM and at times the volume is so great that it no longer functions as an effective method of communication. Another disadvantage of e-mail is that it tends to be curt and has none of the body-language messages attached to it. Time spent in reading and answering mail means less time available to spend in the company of the team.

Teams are a social entity and they need time together. Conference calls can provide a good vehicle but to avoid telephone tag they are scheduled, and therefore lack spontaneity. Video conferencing allows members to see one another, but depending on the size of the group and the quality of the video, everyone might not participate.

Face-to-face meetings are crucial. Fortunately, IBM recognizes that investment in such meetings is critical to the success of the team. In these meetings, everyone can see information on white boards or flip charts; asking questions is easier, and members can read the more subtle body-language messages. For this project, meetings rotate between sites, helping every site to feel part of the team and part of the decision-making process. Not everyone attends all meetings but everyone attends some meetings. These meetings build trust within teams and between teams. They prevent the "out-of-sight, out-of-mind" problem and allow the vision to be repeated and reinforced and, at times, celebrated.

Each of these mechanisms for communication is valuable and must be balanced because of the cost of time and money. However, during times of crisis or difficulty, face-to-face meetings prove to be so important that team members must learn how to conduct effective meetings, and have trained meeting leaders throughout the organization. We are still learning this lesson.

In asking several members what we could do better, the response was: "State where we are going, don't churn on it, get there and celebrate the journey."

# KEY LEARNINGS

## THE REQUIREMENTS FOR SUCCESSFUL VIRTUAL TEAMS

- Face-to-face meetings whenever possible
- A clearly articulated mandate and vision
- The consistent and frequent communication of direction
- Members who have a sense of personal responsibility and comfort with the new culture
- Clearly understood accountabilities and agreements as to outcomes if commitments are not met
- Individual performance evaluations tied to team outcomes
- A commitment to making communication a priority

*Most of these success factors apply to any team. They are more critically important for the virtual team.*

# 11

# A NEW FOCUS ON
# TEAMS AT THE TOP

The debate over whether teaming at the top is feasible has been a popular one in human resource management circles. The argument against putting effort into developing the teams at the top is that people who reach the peak, or near the peak, of the organization are by nature competitive drivers — a hopeless bunch, it is assumed, when it comes to teamwork. Never could they set aside personal agendas long enough to become part of a cohesive team. Whether the argument has any validity no longer matters. Legitimate teams at the top are a necessity in the new organization. The new kind of team at the top needs a much greater degree of interconnectedness than did the traditional management "team." In addition to fulfilling the organization's mandate, the senior management team has two key purposes.

*1.To produce the organizational wisdom that will guide the organization through an endlessly unpredictable terrain*
    This includes ensuring the organization knows what information is necessary to its success and has the mechanisms to collect, disperse and apply it.

*2. To create a relevant value-based culture, a culture that works in the new economy*
From a simple bottom-line perspective, this purpose is essential because ethics are becoming a measure against which businesses are assessed by the consumer. Quality, a good price and a smile are important to consumers but they aren't enough any longer. As life becomes more complicated, people look for something they can count on and their expectations are high.

Inside the organization we need highly committed people. Some suggest that people just aren't committed any more. I believe that it's not that people don't want to be committed; they need something worthwhile to be committed to. A principle-based culture is good for business and energizes employees.

## THEORY IN ACTION

Although management groups were perhaps the first to adopt the "team" label, relatively few have made an effort to develop and work as a team. It is often assumed that senior managers have the skills, or should have the skills, and therefore the skills are being applied. Or just as often, the group is so focused on task that there is no recognition of the degree to which lack of teamwork negatively affects outcomes.

A few organizations who are leaders in their industry and intend to stay there, and others who are determined to get there, have recognized the importance of developing the management team. One of those forward-thinking organizations is Unum Canada.

Managers at Unum Canada, like most groups of managers, had been ignoring the team process. They were a highly capable group of professionals committed to excellence and were dealing with an enormous amount of change. Individually, they had managed to continue to achieve in spite of the changes and the resulting heavy work load. However, as changes escalated, the need to work together more effectively became apparent. They were a talented group of people who had not been tapping their collective potential, and they had found evident cracks in the team's group process.

The following four steps were critical to the growth the team experienced in the team development process.

*1. Developing a collective team profile and personal task/process profiles [see pages 44 and 56] was a key factor to members' better understanding how the team worked.*
The team's profile described a highly task-oriented group with predominantly convergent thinkers. This had contributed to their success as efficient managers, who were good decision makers and could be depended upon to make it happen. On the other hand, members frequently held firm opinions; telling and discussing had been the most common modes of communication; dialoguing seldom occurred and group-process issues were ignored. The team members realized that by better balancing their attention to task and attention to process they could enhance their already strong performance. The team developed a set of working agreements to help ensure its good intentions became actions.

*2. Reclarifying roles was essential as corporate changes had blurred parameters and some roles were in a state of transition.*

*3. Redefining its purpose as the management team in the context of the changing organization refocused the group.*
As is usually the case when managers are challenged by change, members had been giving most of their attention to the management of the pieces. Redefining their purpose shifted members' attention to the whole. It also increased cohesiveness by giving the group a stronger and clearer shared vision.

*4. Identifying the team's critical success factors and developing strategies for managing them was essential.*
Critical success factors are the few areas that must be well managed if success is to be achieved. They are unique to each team and its organization at this particular time and place. The Unum team members asked, "What factors are critical to our fulfilling our purpose in the long and short terms?" They identified several success factors including:
1. Communicating effectively with specific groups and individuals;
2. Managing an effective business plan;
3. Continuing the team development process.

The managers realized that team development is not an event but an ongoing process. A team can never assume it has arrived!

What the team did in its development process was important, but would not have created substantive change without team members' commitment. This included a commitment of highly valuable time and, perhaps even more difficult, commitment to make personal adjustments as needed and to live by the agreements the team selected as essential to its success. Within a short time the team had better balanced its attention to task and to process and had increased considerably its level of team performance. Team effectiveness measurements quickly showed an impressive improvement.

Kathryn Yates, vice-president and general manager, and champion of the team process, ties improved business performance to the evident increased level of team performance. In addition, the team worked effectively on strategic matters, positioning the company well for continued success.

Management teams that maintain a task focus are unlikely to develop the wisdom and generate the energy that the new organization requires to thrive.

# 12

# TEAM LEARNING

Members of the new organization participate in each of the new types of teams. The success of the new organization depends on its members' ability to come together quickly and effectively as a team and to juggle their commitment to many teams.

It wasn't long ago that many team-development theorists were suggesting that it takes considerable time, even years, for a team to fully develop. If that were true, teams would be completely incompatible with today's fast-paced environment. Successful teams have learned that managing their development can produce growth spurts and speed up the process. The new kind of team requires an even more accelerated development process. Learning and using an accelerated process does not have to be an onerous task. Its components are quite basic.

## TEAMWORK SKILLS

All members of the organization require a kit of common teamwork skills, facilitation skills and common teamwork methodologies that they carry from team to team. When team members all have teamwork know-how, speak a common teamwork language and arrive with similar expectations of the process, the team quickly becomes productive. A secondary benefit is that team knowledge held by each member leads to shared leadership and greater self-direction.

## Dialogue

The most critical skill is dialoguing. Dialogue, unfortunately, is in danger of becoming a buzzword, likely to create a flurry of "how to dialogue" workshops and then be pushed aside by the next new idea. Dialogue is not new and is too important to be trendy. It's more than a communication technique; it is the essence of communication. It is the trigger for and means of maintaining all interconnectedness.

The communication that takes place in most interactions is sometimes referred to as dialoguing, but is usually discussion. Discussion is a vertical form of communication. This may sound contradictory as the intent of communication is horizontal, and is usually meant to form a connection between two or more people. However, it often doesn't.

In discussion, the participants view their primary responsibility as clearly presenting their point of view and convincing others of its correctness. It is the other person's responsibility to convince them otherwise. Discussion is the display of various pieces of information or perceptions rather than a forum for using them as a springboard to greater things.

Dialogue at its highest level requires a very different perspective on the role of individuals in communication processes and how information and knowledge can most powerfully be used. In dialogue, participants are cognizant of their dual responsibility — that of clearly presenting information or points of view they hold and understanding the information and points of view presented by others. In dialogue it is not individuals, but the body of knowledge created by the group, that influences the participants, and, ultimately, the outcomes.

Dialogue is not meant to replace discussion, but to complement and augment it. In most groups, the entire process takes place in a discussion mode. The results are mediocre decisions and little consensus.

An effective group balances vertical and horizontal behaviors and moves comfortably back and forth between discussion and dialogue. In a decision-making process, for example, a group would use dialogue to share information, explore it, and ensure it is thoroughly understood. In the discussion mode, ideas that had come from the dialogue would be examined, weighed, and then the decision would be made. The result? Quality decisions and commitment to make them work (see Figure 12.1).

Figure 12.1

## DISCUSSION AND DIALOGUE

### DISCUSSION
Convergent behavior

### DIALOGUE
Divergent behavior

- Presenting ideas/opinions (telling)
- Holding one's own position
- Coming to closure

- Questioning, probing for information
- Opening to others' points of view/ information
- Setting aside personal assumptions

In a highly effective decision-making process, the group moves back and forth between discussion and dialogue. Dialogue ensures full understanding of one another's points of view and the development of an unbiased and rich body of information which the group will use to make its decision. Discussion supports the analysis of the body of information, decison making and closure.

Dialogue requires learning how to increase individual and group awareness of task/process balance; how to recognize and set aside personal biases that could block dialogue and how to probe for greater understanding. The most exciting aspect of dialoguing is that the skills are relatively simple to learn. Some argue that dialoguing won't happen without a foundation of trust and trust takes time to develop. That is like suggesting that we have to trust that we won't drown if we are to learn to swim. If we kick our feet hard enough and use a few basic strokes.

### Facilitation Skills
The other essential in the tool kit is a set of basic facilitation skills. In the new organization every member of the organization puts together and leads Need-Driven Teams. How much is accomplished will be reflected in the facilitator's ability to support the group in finding its task/process

balance. When I ask managers to calculate a rough estimate of the number of hours spent in team meetings and the annual cost, most are shocked.

When we consider the dollar investment in meetings and, more important, that this is where the success of the organization is determined, it is shocking how little investment is made in improving the quality of meetings.

## A Team-Development System

Organizations need a common team-development system that each team automatically initiates, including an up-front kick-start session. This ensures that the team balances its attention to task and attention to the team process. Managing the team process must become part of the team's job.

The team process is often ignored because people don't have the knowledge to recognize its importance; the task oriented members resist the idea of spending time on process rather than the task at hand; the team is already overloaded and is often dealing with emergencies. There is never enough time. Team meetings in which team members look at the way they work together are like a sports team's practice and chalkboard sessions in which players learn one another's capabilities, learn what to expect from one another and plan how they will work together.

Imagine an NHL hockey team stepping on the ice ready for a game with no rules for the game, having had no practices, and no chalkboard strategizing. We would not expect it to perform, let alone win the Stanley Cup. Yet organizations put their work groups on the ice every day and expect them to win with few, if any, rules of the team game, no practices and no team strategy.

Initially there needs to be dual emphasis on both team members' skill development and team development because most organizations are in a catch-up position — few have implemented team learning across the organization. As more members learn the skills and tools, teams will develop much more quickly and function more effectively with less need for outside intervention.

Team development can happen only when a team takes responsibility for its growth and ongoing team process. This means pausing to self-examine its present level of effectiveness, identifying opportunities for growth, making commitments to actions that will ensure that growth and constantly reviewing progress (see Figure 12.2).

Figure 12.2

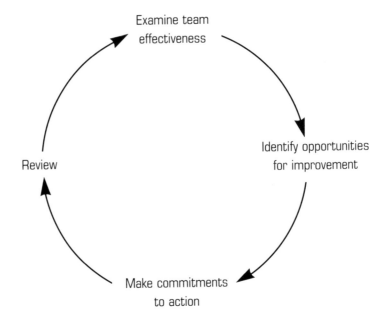

Team development is an ongoing, continuous process that requires each team member's participation in these four steps for effective teamwork.

# THE SIMPLEST BUT THE TOUGHEST

The most commonly cited block to teamwork effectiveness is lack of trust. When the causes of lack of trust are discussed, two are most often cited: poor communication and assumptions about others and their actions.

The English language has many inadequacies. In addition, many people do not communicate effectively, particularly if the issue being discussed is sensitive. Opportunities to misunderstand and be misunderstood are plentiful.

A great deal of effort is spent in trying to ensure that others understand us and a great amount of distress is experienced when they do not. If we could more easily get to know one another as people, we would not have to try so hard to make the connections — they would just happen.

Some Native peoples' communities had a tradition that, combined with their value of accepting individuals as they were, simplified getting to know one another. Each individual at birth was given a shield that represented who he or she was. The animals, plants and elements depicted represented the individual's personal characteristics.

A story is told of a Southwestern tribe which for hundreds of years followed the custom of hanging an individual's shield on his or her teepee. It is said that during this whole period, there was no conflict or war. There could be no misunderstanding; everyone knew and accepted the others' idiosyncrasies. For example, if someone were of the cougar people, it would be known that when cougar people lose their balance, they can be fierce toward anyone that they feel has wounded them, or if the individual is of the deer people, it would be known that the individual is not comfortable talking about herself or himself. People responded to others according to their characteristics. There was an effort to respect individuals' uniqueness and to hold realistic expectations of them. Individuals did not expect another person to respond as they themselves would have. This did not mean that people were not expected to grow, but that it was each individual's responsibility to recognize the need.

Picture an office full of work stations. At every work station hangs a personal emblem or shield that depicts in pictures the characteristics or makeup of the individual who occupies the work station. At a quick glance you would know whether the person works well under pressure, prefers to do several things simultaneously, can unintentionally be curt if approached when busy or is highly task focused and may forget to communicate.

We often cannot transfer practices from one culture to another or from one environment to another; however, very often there are important underlying principles that are universal.

The key learnings from the power shields are the benefits of:
1. Getting to know co-workers better as people;
2. Accepting individual differences;
3. Recognizing our personal responsibilities as members of a system;
4. Adjusting our behaviors, when necessary, for the betterment of the system.

These might sound like another set of nice human-resource values, but they deserve closer examination.

Getting to know one another can easily be encouraged in an organization, and the payoff is huge: recognizing others' strengths that can be tapped; developing a comfort level in connecting with one another; a greater likelihood of Spontaneous Teams in which the highest quality ideas can be produced; an increased willingness to take risks because fear of what others think is lessened. The list goes on.

An environment that sets people free to be themselves and to think independently unleashes energy, commitment and creativity. Mission and value statements, teams and their credos are all meant to create a direction and framework within which individual strengths can be tapped.

I have had the pleasure of a few experiences in which the appreciation for individual differences and the right to those differences was evident. One of these, not surprisingly, occurred during a workshop with a group of Native people. Everyone arrived in the morning in a leisurely fashion and gathered around a large table in a room with an L-shaped alcove. The last member to arrive strolled past the group, a newspaper under his arm, and settled in one of the chairs that lined the walls of the alcove. As the rest of us began workshop discussions, he opened his newspaper which he perused — or at least went through the motions of perusing — for most of the morning. There were no furtive glances in his direction, no hushed side conversations, and the leader did not take him aside at break. He was left to do what, for whatever reason, he felt he needed to do. In late morning he pulled a chair up to the table and became a full participating member of the group. He had made his own decision that the process was useful and he became committed to it.

In a workshop with a senior management team, the group struggled to come to agreement on the definition of consensus for their team. The company, as has been the norm in the nineties, was doing some major refocusing, and the management team wanted to be prepared as a group for the increasingly difficult challenges ahead.

Several VPs were adamant that once there had been open discussion, airing of differences and as much give and take on issues as possible within their meetings, the team must leave the meeting room with one voice. Some wanted agreement that this indeed would be the way the team would operate. One or two were insistent that they could not agree to supporting all decisions made by the team. Finally, one vice-president turned to the CEO who had been very quiet and asked, "Don't you expect us to leave here in one voice?" "No," he responded. "I want us to work toward consensus. If we don't reach it, I want everyone to leave this room feeling free to express whatever they feel is appropriate. I don't want anyone to feel they are expected to toe the party line."

When I share this example with groups, some people see it as courageous and enlightened leadership; others call it naively idealistic. Freedom to choose results in energetic commitment from supporters rather than reluctant compliance. However, encouraging people to be true to themselves and to do what they believe to be best brings positive outcomes when individuals have the good of the organization and the team at heart, and they are in concert with the organization's values and priorities.

Most important, individuals must see themselves as part of a system, recognizing the impact their actions have on the system and being accountable for them. They recognize their influence on the greater whole but also that if it is healthy, they can be healthy.

## PERSONAL RESPONSIBILITY

Freedom to act independently in the organization comes with responsibilities. Individuals' decisions must be principle driven. Self-direction works best when the organization has a clear sense of self that is compatible with the individual sense of self. The principles that guide the organization, its mission and vision must be clear, and members must be able to not only comply but commit to them. This can happen only if the principles are specific enough to form criteria for decision-making processes. They must be active in every process and reflected in each decision.

Keeping values alive and integrating them into behavior requires regular reminders as well as measurement, exemplified by Unum's People Goals, which we examined earlier. In the Unum People Goals process, employees measure the degree to which their work unit is demonstrating Unum values by responding to a series of statements such as: "In my work unit, we work well with people who have different styles, values and/or opinions." "In my work unit, taking initiative is valued and rewarded." People are challenged to ask themselves not only "Do we *believe* in these values?" but also "Do we *demonstrate* this belief?"

In addition to having commitments to corporate principles, the self-directed team and individual must examine their own ethical responsibility in the workplace. Accepting responsibility within a principles-focused organization means making ethically based decisions.

Members must learn that with power comes responsibility. They must make decisions thoughtfully with the acute awareness that they are working in a system and every decision sends ripples outward.

L. Nash proposes a set of Questions for Examining the Ethics for Business Decisions that could be adopted by all employees. Yassin Sankar recommends them in *Value-Based Management for the Information Society*.

1. Have you defined the problem accurately?
2. How would you define the problem if you stood on the other side of the fence?
3. How did this situation occur in the first place?
4. To whom and to what do you give your loyalty as a person and as a member of the corporation?
5. What is your intention in making this decision?
6. How does this intention compare with the probable results?
7. Whom could your decision or action injure?
8. Can you discuss the problem with the affected parties before you make your decision?
9. Are you confident that your position will be as valid over a long period of time as it seems now?
10. Could you disclose, without qualm, your decision or action to your boss, your CEO, the board of directors, your family, society as a whole?
11. What is the symbolic potential of your action if understood? If misunderstood?
12. Under what conditions would you allow exceptions to your stand?

Creating the organization in which individuals are optimally self-directed takes the two commodities many organizations are shortest of — time and money. Money, partly because time is money but also because investment in employee development is essential in creating the new organization. The other requirement is follow-through, traditionally an organizational weakness.

Although the components are basic, many organizations will not make the commitments necessary to ensure the creation of a team-based organization in which individual and team learning are treated as critical success factors. Those organizations will not have the flexibility, responsiveness and wisdom to thrive in the new economy.

The other required commitment is to put mechanisms in place to grow a culture that emphasizes the values of interconnectedness and knowledge. If these values are not in place, it is unlikely that members will be able to take full advantage of the teamwork opportunities. (This assumes that the culture already reflects a belief in empowerment, inclusivity and quality. If not, these need to be added and the organization is in a catch-up position.)

A few organizations have a head start as for several years they have been supporting their members in developing many of the required skills and in changing the culture. One of the best known is GE, an example mentioned in chapter 4. When Jack Welch arrived at GE in the early eighties, he restructured and then quickly turned to creating a new culture. He recognized the need to balance vertical and horizontal activities and behaviors. A more open culture in which information is shared and members are expected to think and question was developed. The GE story frequently grabbed the cover or lead story of business magazines, partly because Welch is the type of person who gets attention but also because the story deserved telling. It was an example of cultural change — which can be too slow — happening with energy and relative speed.

Cultural change requires several simultaneous and ongoing interventions, and GE had all of the required pieces for successful change: commitment at the top, which not only creates energy but ensures the dollar commitment necessary for success; senior management modeling the new behavior; learning opportunities throughout the organization; clear expectations demonstrated through planned activities. GE became particularly known for its workouts — sessions attended by managers and their staff at which management could be asked any questions. Managers were given a limited amount of time in the session to either respond or make a commitment to getting back to the group after the session within a specific time. These workouts required new behaviors on the part of everyone and made it clear that the new way of working was not just being talked about, nor was it the flavor of the week. It was not going to go away and people were expected to *do* things differently.

# REFLECTION & APPLICATION

Do your meetings help strengthen interconnectedness? Use these questions to evaluate your team meetings.

1. Check for dialogue by counting the number of probing questions that are asked. A probing question is aimed at achieving better understanding. For example: "I'm not sure I understood that — could you explain further?" Not "What were the stats on the latest test?" If there are no, or few, probing questions, you are discussing. Missing the dialogue component limits interconnectiveness and can undermine the quality of outcomes.

2. Do you balance attention to task and process in your meetings? Do you set aside time to examine how the team works together?

3. How often have you participated in Spontaneous Teamwork (for a definition, see page 121), which contributed to outcomes in the past two weeks? If Spontaneous Teamwork happens frequently and well (effective outcomes and including the right people), it suggests strong interconnectedness.

# 13

# FORGING UNLIKELY PARTNERSHIPS

Partnerships traditionally are formed by people with complementary assets and a common vision, who see benefit in working together to fulfill that vision. Some creative strategic partnerships are still formed on that basis. Other partnerships are being forged out of necessity.

The fast-paced, short-lived, competitors-at-our-heels type of innovation requires tapping the best minds available, even if they are not part of our own organization. They may even be competitors.

Public-sector industries such as Canadian health care, to whom competition has been a foreign concept, now often find themselves either directly or indirectly competing. Public-nursing organizations, such as the Victorian Order of Nurses, must compete with new private nursing services. As hospitals close, there is an element of the survival of the fittest at play. Drastic funding cuts prevent hospitals from providing the superior quality of care they believe in and in which they have always taken pride. Most have turned to partnerships to help protect the quality of the health-care system, if not their own facilities. The process tests even the most altruistic participants.

The scenarios created often lack the partnership foundation pieces, trust and a shared vision of something better than the present. Adding to the complexity is the belief in the participation of stakeholders.

In the new economy, an even greater emphasis on participation and self-direction will be driven by several currently recognized principles: the people who do the job are the experts and their contribution is essential to the best decisions; stakeholders have a right to be involved; people who plan the battle (the change or decision) don't battle the plan, meaning that people with a vested interest in a decision or process will be motivated to make it work; more perspectives bring richer decisions; most people and groups of people, given the right skills and structure, are capable of self-management.

These principles are obviously positive and valuable. At the same time, if the participation process is not well managed it can hinder the partnership. The result can be too many participants, often with different agendas — not the ingredients for consensus.

In 1985 IBM and Microsoft became partners in designing and implementing the OS/2. The partnership not only failed but resulted in a rift between two companies that each had much to gain from co-operation. It was also a huge and costly partnership. Why did it fail? According to Bill Gates, primarily because of different visions and too much participation. Microsoft wanted to create the best possible PC operating software. IBM saw a system whose applications would be compatible with its mainframe and mid-range systems. The two visions were not compatible.

More recently, IBM has entered into various successful partnerships — IBM suggests that this is due to its learning to let go and let partners manage what they do best.

Centuries ago, the Iroquois displayed a great deal of wisdom in developing a system for the formation of a highly unlikely partnership. The Iroquois were warring tribes. Their enmity and the constancy of the fighting and atrocities had meant no peace or prosperity for many years. In *Heeding the Voices of Our Ancestors*, Gerald R. Alfred decribes how a peacemaker facilitated a process through which the separate tribes came together to form the Iroquois Nation. The Nation would be ruled by the Kaienerekowa, or the Great Law, a value-based set of laws that applied to government and social organization. The nation was governed by consensus and participation. The chief's role was to rule by the consensual will of the people.

The role of the chief was to determine the will of his people and communicate it to the league and to be a moral and spiritual leader. "Their spirits want for the good of their people; the spirits of anger and fury shall not find place in them, and in everything they say and do they will think only of the [people] and not of themselves, thinking ahead not only of the present but also of the generations of unborn yet to come."

The Iroquois experience may not parallel all of our modern, unlikely partnerships but the value-based laws they adopted to forge the partnerships would aid many. It was expected that:

- Individual differences would be accepted and appreciated;
- Decisions would be made through participation and consensus;
- Each nation would be self-directed and autonomous;
- Each would govern itself by the laws of the creator.

A basic Iroquois belief, rooted in the creation story, is that people are equal but inescapably different. Differences are accepted. At the core of the Great Law is the belief that self-determination and national autonomy provide the only guarantees of peaceful coexistence.

Each was to be given self-direction and autonomy, *but* govern itself by the laws of the creator. In other words, there was self-direction within specific parameters. For modern partnerships these parameters would be determined by the agreed-upon purpose and a team's working agreements and/or set of principles.

# THEORY IN ACTION

Lack of common vision, trust and ineffective participation consistently appear as the stumbling blocks in partnerships that run into difficulty.

Challenging partnerships were formed when Ontario decided to restructure the way in which long-term care services were delivered. Committees were struck across the province to design a delivery model for their own communities.

The task of these highly diverse committees was to do the unthinkable: create an entirely new long-term care delivery model so different that it was likely that some of the present delivery organizations, many of whom had representatives sitting at the table, would no longer exist.

The members of the group I would eventually have the opportunity of working with dived into the task with trepidation, but with enormous commitment to ensuring quality service to their community and a determination to do whatever might be necessary to fulfill their mandate to the best of their ability.

The makeup of the committee demonstrated the belief in full stakeholder participation and ownership. One-third of the members were consumers who accessed long-term care services, one-third service providers and one-third "others," which could include members of municipal governments, women's groups, seniors' councils, labor groups or other sectors of the community. The complexity and sensitive nature of the group's task, combined with the size (23 people) and highly diverse makeup of the group, predestined the committee to tough challenges.

The best of altruistic intentions could not remove all personal and professional paradigms that dictated for each member his or her perceptions of what would work and what would not, what was best for the community and what wasn't. Trust was a major issue. Suggestions made by service deliverers, for example, were often suspect. Why were they suggesting this, others wondered — for the good of the community or for the benefit of the organization they represented? Many members of the group were highly process oriented with a need to discuss and work through issues. The result was a group that was so highly process oriented that it experienced frustration and a sense of wheel spinning because insufficient task orientation and the structure that goes with it meant the group process was initially not well managed.

Most members were sensitive, highly feeling individuals, which resulted in their frequently not dealing with important issues for fear of hurting someone's feelings. Recognizing these natural tendencies by developing a team task/process profile was an important step for the group. It led to the members' coming to agreement on changes the group needed to make in its behaviors and *modus operandi*. Examining their Success Potential provided other important insights (see Figure 14.1).

# EVALUATING SUCCESS POTENTIAL

A group's success potential depends on the difficulty or complexity of the task at hand and the degree of natural cohesiveness of the group. Here we are defining success potential as the ability to complete the task at hand.

Figure 14.1

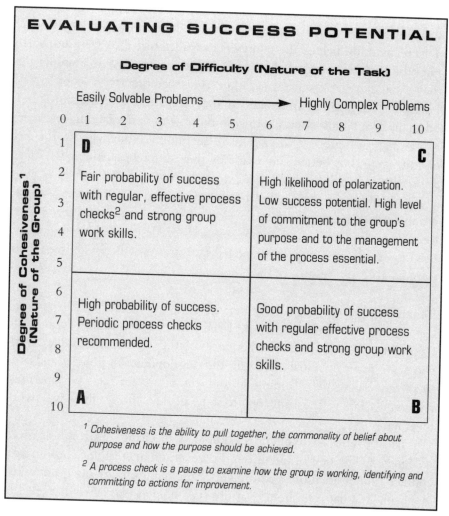

**EVALUATING SUCCESS POTENTIAL**

**Degree of Difficulty (Nature of the Task)**

Easily Solvable Problems ⟶ Highly Complex Problems

0   1   2   3   4   5   6   7   8   9   10

**Degree of Cohesiveness[1] (Nature of the Group)**

**D**

Fair probability of success with regular, effective process checks[2] and strong group work skills.

**C**

High likelihood of polarization. Low success potential. High level of commitment to the group's purpose and to the management of the process essential.

**A**

High probability of success. Periodic process checks recommended.

**B**

Good probability of success with regular effective process checks and strong group work skills.

[1] Cohesiveness is the ability to pull together, the commonality of belief about purpose and how the purpose should be achieved.

[2] A process check is a pause to examine how the group is working, identifying and committing to actions for improvement.

A group of like-minded customer-service people, for example, who work closely together, have some basic group-work skills and are charged with designing a customer-service questionnaire, should be able to accomplish their task quite easily. If they are evaluating their Success Potential, they might position themselves at a 9 on the degree of cohesiveness scale and at a 2 on the degree of difficulty scale. That puts them in quadrant A, which suggests they have a high probability of success.

The long-term care committee quickly placed itself in quadrant C, seeing itself at 1 on the cohesiveness scale and 10 on the complexity scale. This recognition helped the members to realize that they were not solely responsible for frustrations they were experiencing. It wasn't simply that they "couldn't get their act together" but that they were coping with highly challenging circumstances. If they were to succeed against these odds, the group must continue to commit time to understanding and managing the group process. In particular, they must compensate for the lack of cohesiveness by better understanding their differences, members' styles, the team's style and by developing working agreements.

Eventually the group's mandate was adjusted to match better what the group could best contribute to develop a plan for long-term care services for the coming year. Decision-making sessions designed with the group's need for well-managed process and led by a strong facilitator allowed them to move toward the success they deserved.

## Learnings

- A new committee has replaced the original Long-Term Care Committee. Based on the experience of the earlier committee it has chosen to focus its initial efforts on the development of policies and protocols governing the planning of long-term care services. Groups must commit to taking the time up front to decide "how" they will work together.
- The benefits of involving stakeholders in change processes are well recognized. The best of intentions, however, often create nonproductive, conflict-ridden situations because very basic questions are often not asked in advance. What role should various stakeholders play? At what level of empowerment can they best contribute — making the final decision, contributing input to the decision or contributing criteria for making the decision?

Once a draft of the possible makeup of a decision-making body has been put together, ask some questions: Is it possible for this group to reach a consensus? Do we have sufficient cohesiveness, maturity and group-process skills? If not, can we compensate for the weaknesses or do we have the wrong group? The answer might be: We have the "wrong" group in its ability to work effectively toward consensus, but we have no choice. In that case, it is essential to ensure:

1. a highly experienced facilitator;
2. an emphasis on team development;
3. an agreement on how the decision will be made if consensus cannot be reached;
4. that members have or develop the required skills.

• In order for unlikely partnerships to thrive, we need all of the basics discussed earlier. But they are not enough. In a very complex and challenging process, a simple foundation is essential. There must be some things people can count on: respect for one another, an acceptance of differences, and an agreement on principles that are actively used as a scale in weighing decisions and as the compass in determining direction.

---

# REFLECTION & APPLICATION

## Building Partnerships — A Checklist

Building partnerships requires:

❑ Agreeing on purpose
*Don't assume understanding of purpose. Spell it out. If you can't get agreement on purpose early on, reconsider the partnership.*

❑ Finding the appropriate membership
*To make consensus possible, members will need the required technical skills, knowledge and experience and the required group-process skills.*

❑ Agreeing on roles and expectations
*This includes who does what, who has what authority, what contributions are expected from each member of the partnership.*

❑ Checking the success potential (see page 151)
*Check the partnership's success potential and provide whatever supports are required. These may include:*
    • *facilitation skills;*

- *initial focusing and team-development sessions;*
- *ongoing development as needed.*

❏ Examining and understanding the differences
*This is particularly important if the cohesiveness level is low. Even if differences cannot be resolved, bringing them to light and openly discussing them lessens their power to inhibit the process.*

❏ Capitalizing on commonalities
*Find areas team members agree on and build on these.*

❏ Avoiding assumptions
*This is a broad statement and can apply to various aspects of partnering but refers particularly to ensuring common understanding. Jargon can be used very differently in different organizations/sectors/industries, or even departments. Apparently simple words such as "program," "timetable" and "team" can have very different meanings to different groups.*

❏ Getting to know one another

❏ Seeing crisis as an opportunity for renewal when partnering under duress

# Part IV

# CREATING ENERGY

For many organizations, an all-consuming, bottom-line focus and organizational anorexic tendencies have been self-destructive. The organization is living on whatever energy its emotionally and physically exhausted employees can muster. Their energy is not being renewed and will eventually be depleted.

Energy depletion is a critical issue for most organizations. How long can we keep running to catch up, keep up, get ahead and stay ahead?

# 14

# KEEPING BODY AND SOUL TOGETHER

Many companies have been so focused on keeping the body together that they have forgotten the soul. The result is the energy crisis so many organizations are facing.

Energy reserves are nonexistent and fuel cannot be purchased. It has to be created from within, but few organizations are tending to energy renewal. Some organizations have experienced knife wielders so focused on the bottom line that they don't see the people; they cut out not only the fat but the soul of the organization. In others, preoccupation with the bottom line, the pressure of global competition and overwork mean little time or interest in renewal.

There are, on the other hand, organizations that, in spite of high expectations and heavy work loads, have high levels of energy. Visitors to Enterprise Systems Inc., described earlier, frequently comment on the high level of energy they feel in the organization. Its source, according to management, is members' exceptional level of commitment to doing the job well and the pride they take in their products, service and client relationships. Abraham Maslow might have referred to the members of Enterprise Systems Inc. as self-actualized, as experiencing their personal potential.

In the past when energy level was low in the organization, management would look for means to motivate the employees. Motivation was a hot topic for decades, challenging people to think about carrot-versus-stick management, human-relations versus human-resource management. Maslow's hierarchy of needs was the model most commonly used in "how to motivate your employees" workshops. In our high-tech world of almost instant obsolescence, anything not brand new is often considered irrelevant. It is common to discard important knowledge. Maslow's hierarchy has a good deal of relevance in the new organization.

Maslow applied the following descriptions to the hierarchy of human needs.

**Physiological Needs**
Physiological needs are met by food and shelter — within the organization by salary and benefits.

**Safety Needs**
Most simply, Maslow describes safety as not being in danger, but goes on to add that "other broader aspects of the attempt to seek safety and stability in the world are seen in the very common preference for familiar rather than unfamiliar things or for the known rather than the unknown."

**Love Needs**
Maslow describes love needs as a need for love, affection and belonging.

**Esteem Needs**
He describes esteem needs this way: "All people in our society (with a few pathological exceptions) have a need or desire for a stable, firmly based (usually), high evaluation of themselves for self-respect or self-esteem and for the esteem of others. By firmly based self-esteem we mean that which is soundly based upon real capacity, achievement and respect of others."

**Self-Actualization Needs**
The need for self-actualization refers to the desire for self-fulfillment, namely, the tendency for the individual to become actualized in his or her potential. "This tendency might be phrased as the desire to become more and more what one is to become; everything that one is capable of becoming."

Maslow's theory suggests that if a person is hungry, all energy will be focused on getting food. Being self-actualized has no meaning to the hungry person; therefore, each level of need must be met in hierarchical order. The ultimate need will be recognized and therefore must be met once the other more basic needs have been met.

Unfortunately, organizations became so focused on the lower needs — physiological safety — that most did not effectively meet the higher needs. The love needs were met in some organizations that created a sense of belonging. This is easiest in small start-up operations, early Apple or Microsoft, for example. If someone is to feel a sense of belonging, there has to be something to belong to. Something with a clear identity and something one can be proud of.

One of the reasons organizations were stuck at the lower need levels of motivation was that employees' values — at least, the values that were at the forefront of their minds — were upward mobility and consumerism. How much could one make, and how quickly, in order to buy the new house or car, or, more likely, pay down the debt on the new house or car? Position and power within the organization, and the salary attached to them, represented one's degree of success, and self-esteem came through promotions, titles, 10-year pins and 25-year watches.

As corporations reorganize around teams, and managers become either leaders or specialists within the teams, people are sometimes reluctant to let go of the image of power. One individual disclosed that it had been months before he told his family and friends that he was no longer a manager. The label of team leader did not carry with it the influence and power of the manager label.

The new organization can no longer meet and surpass the lower needs as in the past. Salary and benefits are capped and, in fact, many have been cut and are unlikely to grow quickly. Although physical safety is a priority for most large companies, particularly in manufacturing, the other safety requirement described by Maslow — "a preference for familiar rather than unfamiliar things or for the known rather than the unknown" — is almost impossible to meet when change is constant (we can, however, better support people through the change process and so alleviate some of the stress attached to the fact that this need cannot be fully met). A team-based organization means little upward movement and few titles, and workers are often referred to as associates, members or partners, with no role distinction.

In the new organization, individuals must take greater responsibility for their own physiological and safety needs. The organization will, of course, continue to provide income and benefits but it may not fully satisfy the physiological and safety needs of the individual in the latter half of the 1990s. This is a reality because uncertainty and global competition are here to stay. Personal income growth will continue to be more conservative than in the past. Lifetime employment is no longer an expectation. Dealing with these facts of life becomes a responsibility of the individual, and in most cases requires adjusting personal lifestyles and lowering expectations.

The previous focus on physiological needs created imbalance. Organizations did not only ensure that employees' basic needs were met but attempted to satiate a growing hunger for more. During the seventies, eighties and early nineties, upper mobility and consumerism were the main values. However, this addiction to consumerism eventually became depleting, and people began looking inward for meaning. Who am I? What do I have to contribute? How can I express my beliefs in my everyday life? "Old" ideas popular in the sixties, such as meditation, took on new meaning and became adopted by many as a method to enhance the quality of life and define order in chaos.

More people are now looking for more than a paycheck when they come to work. They are no longer willing to check at the door their values, ideas, opinions and sundry talents that may not obviously apply to their job. They know they have more to offer and have a greater need than ever to make a contribution of which they are proud. An organization will never be short of energy if it creates an environment that allows people to be their best.

Work has historically had a negative connotation. People have gone to work to earn a living. "Why are you here?" "To pay the bills," is not an unusual response.

Today the recognition of the need for self-actualization is generally more evident in society and will become even clearer in the organization as the roles of workers change. There have been sporadic efforts over the years to enrich routine manual jobs through such initiatives as sociotech analysis.

It is expected that knowledge workers will gravitate to a specialty that they enjoy (within which they experience joy). The knowledge worker, in particular — although this can be transferred with a little imagination to all roles — has the opportunity to work as a craftsperson. When this happens, there is a tremendous opportunity for self-actualization.

# FROM WORKER TO CRAFTSMAN

The traditional attitude of work as drudgery had its roots in manual labor. Going to work meant going someplace where one worked hard, came home tired but with enough money to provide for a family. For the most part, the laborer did not labor for the love of it.

A very different attitude came from the craftsmen: people who worked (crafted) for the joy of it. Sometimes they earned little, sometimes a great deal if what they produced was superior and they were fortunate enough to be recognized for it.

C.W. Mills describes craftsmanship:

> There is no ulterior motive in work other than the product being made and the processes of its creation. The details of daily work are meaningful because they are not detached in the worker's mind from the product of work. The worker is free to control his own working action. The craftsman is thus able to learn from his work; and to use and develop his capabilities and skills in its prosecution. There is no split of work and play, or work and culture. The craftsman's way of livelihood determines and infuses his entire mode of living.

Note the points in Mills's description that are key to creating the energy that comes from craftsmanship.

*1. The details of daily work are meaningful because they are not detached in the worker's mind from the product of work.*

This aspect is partly dependent on job design, but also on the information the worker has available to him or her and understanding the bigger picture. In the story I cited earlier about the bricklayers, the picture of the cathedral gave meaning to laying bricks. In the new knowledge-and-service based organization, workers need understanding of not only the products and services that they are producing, but how they link to others in the organization to fulfill the organization's mission. Information must be shared generously about what is happening in the organization, and why.

*2. The worker is free to control his own working action.*
The joy created by the ability of the craftsman to self-express and create something of which he or she is proud is in itself powerful, but the sense of freedom that comes from self-direction greatly augments that joy. Even for individuals who may not be working in an area that best taps their talents, self-direction offers opportunity to express themselves by making their own decisions and creating their own outcomes. Shared leadership and self-direction are officially recognized as important values in most organizations. Too few organizations, however, are demonstrating it consistently and effectively.

In most knowledge work in the new organization, self-direction will be inevitable. Knowledge workers will be specialists and will have to respond quickly to the environment around them. The nature of their work will demand that they work in a self-directed mode.

*3. The craftsman is able to learn from his work.*
If there is joy in the work, learning often happens automatically as individuals strive to express the best of themselves. In addition, learning from one's work requires a mind-set that recognizes learning as part of the job. It means taking time for assessment and learning from that assessment. It means valuing information, including input from others. It means that leaders model and expect these behaviors. Yassin Sankar writes:

> To the extent that the worker uses the power of his mind such as insight, imagination, intuition, intelligence, and the aesthetics of the mind, the greater his identification with his work and his pride in his performance. To the extent that work permits creative visualization, problem solving and learning, the greater the challenge in the work and pride in performance.

The job of the organization is to create an environment conducive to the workers' expressing the best of themselves through their work. The workers are, then, responsible for finding, developing and expressing their best.

As people are expected to work more and more independently, to work more with technology and less with people, to work in virtual teams, the members of which may seldom see one another, organizations must make an effort to be sure that the need for love and belonging and self-esteem will be met.

Organizations have been struggling to find forms of recognition that can replace money and position. A small personal recognition such as a "thank you" can mean so much. Even when salary increases were frequent and generous, a common complaint was, "We never hear when we do something right — but boy, just slip up once." People recognize from personal experience the power of small gestures. For example, most of us can remember feeling proud in elementary school when we were asked by the teacher to clean the blackboard, even though most of the other students eventually were asked as well. For that moment we felt a little bit special.

I frequently ask participants in team leadership workshops to describe two instances in the past two weeks when they acknowledged someone's effort with a thanks, a pat on the back, or a job well done. A very large percentage (in many groups none of them) is not able to. They feel embarrassed and annoyed with themselves. They know better, but . . .

Michael A. Stephen, chairman of Aetna International Inc., believes that "we won't prosper in the 21st century unless we celebrate spiritual values in the workplace. A lot of people at work are using 20 percent of their talent. If we could move that up to 40 percent or 60 percent, we couldn't help but be first class. We are in the business to make money, but the way to achieve this is to treat employees with love and respect and we must allow the spirit within to guide that process."

# 15

# THE PRINCIPLE-BASED ORGANIZATION

## ETHICAL CRITERIA

There may be a human need not described by Maslow beyond the need for self-actualization: the need to make a valuable contribution. This gives life meaning. The psychologist Ernst Becker suggested that people don't so much fear extinction but extinction with insignificance. Working according to principles provides significance.

To feel one has made a meaningful contribution requires elements discussed in the last chapter, including:

• Understanding how one's contribution fits into the end product or outcomes;

• Self-direction in making decisions, or at least having the power to influence decisions.

In addition, if people are to feel their work is meaningful, they must believe they are making a contribution to an organization that functions according to principles of which they can be proud. Corporations are being scrutinized from within and without and are being held to high standards.

The reflection that has influenced lifestyle changes has been turned more sharply outward and with a certain amount of anger: "If I'm going to change, the rest of the world had darn well better do something too," is some people's attitude. For others there is a sense of urgency that "This doesn't work anymore — it is not good enough."

Politicians are no longer allowed to say "Read my lips" and later ignore the promise. Corporations continue to be scrutinized for their commitment to the environment and have no option but to respond quickly to criticism or suffer the consequences. Starbucks coffee chain intended to serve the customer better by double-cupping to ensure the paper cups were not too hot to handle comfortably. A loud cry about paper waste stopped the double-cupping. Customers accepted burnt fingers while Starbucks searched for a better cup.

Even corporate profits are suspect. Is there such a thing as too much profit? Are corporations greedy? In the banking industry, the large annual profits, once something to be unveiled with pride, are being announced with almost a sense of embarrassment.

Some people argue that corporate greed cannot exist because profit drives the economy. Profit is expected by shareholders. Profit equals a healthy company, which equals employment. As Albert Dunlop, former CEO of Scott Paper said, "The point of business is to make a profit. Profit, gentlemen, is not a dirty word."

In 1984, IBM set the record for the most money ever made by a firm in a single year, a profit of $6.6 billion. I don't recall greed being an issue then. The Everyman of the day was well employed, and bigger houses, better cars were in his grasp.

Personal economic positions are bound to influence perspectives, but the high ethical standards being set for corporations go beyond this. They go back to the growing recognition that consuming is not enough and that having something that one can trust and believe in is essential. There is a desire for values that are common denominators.

Whether a corporation's profit is labeled greed is not determined by the size of the profit, but the size of the profit measured against the perceived ethics of the organization. Is the organization honest and fair? Greed is determined by people's perception of the answers to the following questions:

• Are employees fairly paid and fairly treated?
• Are the growth of shareholders' dividends outpacing employee earnings?

- Is the corporation generous in its contribution to the community?
- Does the corporation pay its fair share of taxes or does it find off-shore havens?
- Does it treat its customers well and fairly?
- Has it had any questionable business dealings?
- Have executive salaries reached an obscene level while employees' salaries are red-circled or static? How do executive salaries compare to shareholders' earnings?

The media, as well as a long list of watchdogs, closely follow corporate behaviors. We are perhaps most familiar with those who guard the environment. However, corporations are scrutinized by numerous groups. As families have changed from the two-parent, mom-at-home model to two working parents or a single working parent, the stress of balancing home and career has increased. Companies are expected, as ethical corporations, to be putting measures in place to support families better with everything from flextime to on-premises daycare.

The expectation of the corporation to be a good corporate citizen may go beyond ethical behavior. The question is being raised as to whether corporations have a social responsibility. When there is heavy government debt and too high unemployment, should corporations be held responsible for job creation? How high our expectations of corporations will go, or the degree to which their role in society will change, is unclear.

What we do know is that the organization that succeeds in the new economy will set high ethical standards for itself and will live by them. Some companies have a head start. Critics suggest that many are becoming better corporate citizens for purely monetary reasons. Once ethics become a habit, the initial motive will be irrelevant.

When mission statements started appearing in reception areas, they were literally the writing on the wall that the world had changed and corporations had to commit to being good corporate citizens and living by values both inside and outside of the organization. If an organization is truly living by its values, no one has to read its mission statement to know who it is and what it stands for. It expresses itself through every discussion, action and interaction within and without the corporation.

In a team-development workshop in which we were discussing values and mission statements and the demonstration of them, a participant described one of his experiences. "We recently went to visit a friend who was a patient at Women's College Hospital. I noticed a mission statement hanging in the entrance area but didn't pay much attention. When we got to her room, we were blown away by what we saw. Every staff member who came into her room went out of their way to give quality care, show sensitivity and provide exceptional customer service. She said this was what she had experienced the whole time, whether interacting with admission clerks, cleaning staff or medical staff. On our way out, I stopped and looked at the mission statement. After spending a half hour there [in the hospital room] I could have written it!"

Here is the mission and value statement acid test — are the beliefs we espouse part of the fiber of the organization or a false advertisement?

Who we are as individuals or corporations is not defined so much by what we do but how we do it. There are many accounting firms and hamburger chains. *What* we do is usually not unique. *How* we see our role, approach our work and interact with the world around us distinguishes us from the rest.

Decision makers in organizations need clear and easy ethical reference points. M. Guy, cited by Yassin Sankar, suggests using these ethical principles.

1. Treat all human beings with fairness.
2. Do unto others as you would have them do unto you.
3. Act so that your act will produce, over the long range, maximum good.
4. Act so that your act could be made a general law that could be proved from human experience to work toward general human and social success. The question to ask related to this principle is, "Would it still be ethical if everybody did this?"

Setting ethical standards for leaders is another idea that is not new. The Iroquois Great Law held their leaders to ethical principles. The Iroquois chief not only represented his people's interest at the League of Nations, but was also a moral and spiritual leader.

As organizations become more self-directed and the number of individuals making decisions multiplies, the need for a set of ethical criteria for decision making becomes even more important.

When discussing the importance of balance, I referred to the need for companies to establish process-oriented goals as well as task goals. Ethical behaviors fall under the process-oriented goals. Organizations that have already put policy systems and practices in place to support these process goals have a head start.

Companies without a set of ethical decision-making criteria risk not only being perceived as unethical, but having employees actually behaving unethically. White-collar crime by employees is not only embarrassing, but in some cases causes irreparable damage for the company. The Japanese Daiwa Bank was fined $340 million and expelled from the United States because it tried to hide massive bond trading losses by one of its employees.

Texas Instruments has experienced no scandals in its history, and credits its 60-year-old code of conduct. In the late eighties the company set up a full-time ethics office. According to their ethics director, Carl Skooglund, "There were a lot of close calls and a lot of gray areas."

Often companies do not think about ethics until there is a problem and they are trying to retrieve their reputation, or they are terrified of another slip that could be fatal.

When we are functioning in a world that is in shades of gray, full of ambiguities, and with the ground constantly shifting, the chances of making inappropriate decisions either intentionally or unintentionally are high. Clear ethical parameters make life easier and safer. They also increase pride and energy in the organization.

# 16

# "MANAGEMENT" IS NOT A BAD WORD

Political correctness has overtaken the Western world. Fear of offending or of appearing less than "with it" has turned usually articulate people into mumblers and stumblers. The organizational world is not exempt. "Manager," "supervisor" and "employee" have been stricken from the organizational lexicon and replaced with words like "leader," "team member," "associate" and "partner." Words are being seen not as labels but as powerful symbols that not only reflect attitudes but influence them.

The relegation of "manager" to the politically incorrect word heap has somehow also tainted the word "management." Too often, empowerment and self-direction are let loose on the organization and leaders are hesitant to, or don't recognize the need to, ensure that these processes and all others are managed.

Many organizations have leapt into a more process-oriented, self-directed world without providing the structure to support the new models and behaviors. Answers to the essential questions — Who's accountable? and Who has the authority? — are often not clear. When teams appear to be careening off the road, managers are hesitant to intercede for fear of being seen as not walking the talk of empowerment.

Good management has always required structure, including checks and balances. As organizations swing more toward self-direction, more structure, not less, is required to ensure that the job gets done and that people are all pulling in the same direction. The difference in a self-directed environment is that the structures are not imposed from above but are put in place by the team or individual. Those structures that need to be negotiated with management, such as the parameters of authority and performance measurements, will be negotiated. The rest will be determined and applied independently by the team.

The lack of structure and accountability created in many organizations by ineffective moves to a team base is alarming. Elliott Jacques suggests that the move away from the hierarchy is a mistake. His article "In Praise of Hierarchy" acknowledges that "for 300 years the hierarchical organization has not worked," but he believes that rather than replacing it, we must find a way to make it work efficiently. Accountability in a team-based organization is a concern for Jacques. He believes the team-based model avoids the issue of accountability altogether. "For to hold a group accountable, the employment contract would have to be with the group, not with the individual, and companies simply do not employ groups as such."

As the nature of employment quickly evolves, the concept of contracting with the team may no longer be incongruent with the way organizations work. It is already common for groups of internal or external specialists to come together as a team to fulfill a specific and relatively short-term need on a contractual basis. As the new organization progresses in its development, internal teams will work more and more like externally contracted teams. Teams will contract to performance outcomes, and monetary rewards (whether salary bonuses or profit sharing) will more commonly be linked directly to performance — not only individual performance but team performance. Certainly a contract renewal or opportunity for another contract will be based on the quality and timeliness of outcomes produced.

Some organizations have begun to address the accountability issue by tying individual performance assessments, at least in part, to team performance.

Highly self-directed teams, however, are not the only model for success. Traditional teams, those with leaders appointed by the organization, can also effectively support the new organization. In effective traditional teams, members work as self-directedly as their skills, job function and the organization's systems allow. The leader is responsible for ensuring that members work at the highest possible level of self-direction, and there is a focus on the ongoing development of members.

Traditional teams in which members are legitimately empowered are preferable if the organization is not ready or able to put systems in place to make teams accountable. It is not a matter of returning to the old hierarchy and improving it. The old hierarchical organization is not in sync with the new economy. A team-based organization that is well managed is.

## FORM FOLLOWS FUNCTION

The challenge of teams in the new economy has also been a subject of concern to Peter Drucker. He concurs that teams are the basic unit of the organization and requisite to success. Yet he also cites the lack of clear accountability and a frustration over the lack of understanding that there is more than one type of team — there are many variations, depending on the team's function. Drucker uses various analogies to distinguish the types of teams, from jazz combos to sports teams. He suggests that traditional production lines are much like a baseball team in which each player has a distinct role and is responsible for the ball at different times. The Japanese team, however, is more like a soccer team in which all of the team follows the ball down the field.

It may not be productive for a team to analyze the various types of sports teams and try to match itself to one of them, but it is crucial to recognize that form follows function. How a particular team works must be unique to that team, not a copy of another with a different function, even if it appears to work well. The key questions are:
- Who makes what decisions?
- Which decisions need to go to the whole team?
- Which decisions are best made independently by individual members?
- Who should be supporting the decision maker by providing expertise and input?
- Who needs to be kept informed?

In other words, there must be structure — clear definitions of roles and authority by which the team manages. In addition, the overall parameters of authority must be clear.

# STRUCTURE, STRUCTURE AND MORE STRUCTURE

I have repeatedly emphasized the need for balance but have discussed for the most part how to add process-focused practices to the organization's behavioral mix. Interconnectedness, internally and externally, one-on-one or in teams is process oriented; intuition and environmental scanning are process oriented; increasing self-direction and helping individuals self-actualize is process oriented; emphasizing corporate ethics is process oriented.

This chapter is a reminder not to let the pendulum swing too far, but to ensure that balance is achieved while doing all of the above. Sufficient task orientation must be introduced, including: structure, attention to detail, direction, parameters, measurement and closure — good old-fashioned management — but whenever possible (i.e., team has sufficient skills), management from within.

# 17

# FUTURE POSITIVE

In the mid-eighties I decided to focus my practice on organizational change and the teamwork required to support it. When I discussed the need for change management and the fact that organizations needed to be prepared for the even greater change coming, I usually got intellectual agreement, which was often followed by "Does your company do stress management or communication? We have a couple of departments that have got real problems. . . ."

Companies have suffered a great deal more than necessary in the nineties because of their destructive habit of reacting to the immediate needs that cry the loudest, rather than focusing on the bigger picture and preparing for the future.

The need for managing change, open information sharing, shared leadership, high-performance teams and self-directed work forces has been talked about for years. Some companies acted with foresight and began instituting them. Many more went through the motions, such as labeling groups "teams," but never developing them so that any impact that might have been felt was a negative one. Some have done even less as they fought the problem of the day or, in some cases, the problem of the minute.

All of the required practices discussed in previous chapters are essential in functioning well today and tomorrow, but they are not all immediately obvious needs, for example, developing a company's intuition.

We earlier defined the new organization as one that will survive the cross-over and thrive in the new economy. To sustain its success, today's leaders must be aware of potential cracks that are likely to happen because of the nature of the new economy and the nature of the new organization. Then they must put preventive measures in place.

So, it cannot be overstated that the new organization's most important resource and primary asset is knowledge:

• It is team based;
• Many of its teams are virtual or multi-sited teams — in fact, the entire organization may be virtual;
• It is supported primarily by knowledge and service workers;
• Workers are for the most part self-directed;
• Information gathering and continuous learning are highly valued;
• It is humanistic and lives by its code of ethics. This is the highly flexible and responsive organization that is continually reshaping itself to stay in sync with the constantly changing world of the new economy, and it faces new challenges.

# POTENTIAL CRACKS

## The New Divide

In the traditional organization the division was between management and nonmanagement. Management was seen as the élite who held the power. They were in the know and had information and authority. They made "the big bucks," a good reason, nonmanagement argued, for them to be making the decisions and taking the fall if anything went wrong. They also got the perks, the private parking or the corner office with windows.

A great deal of leveling has happened in companies in recent history. The de-layering and downsizing of the first half of the nineties nearly finished the job that began several years before with the introduction of participatory management. CEOs who demonstrated egalitarianism became heroes and the stuff company legends are made of. "Remember the day

Jones started? The first thing he did was to take a bucket of paint, go out to the parking lot and paint out all of the private parking signs." "We knew our new president was going to walk the talk the day he was walking through the plant, spotted something spilled on the floor and went and got a mop and wiped it up himself." Now managers talk about their main function as being a support role to those who get the job done; and many managers sincerely believe it. For many of these leaders, perks that differentiated them from other members of the organization would be an embarrassment.

As knowledge becomes an increasingly important resource, there will be a potential new division in the organization between knowledge workers and "others," most of whom will be service workers.

The knowledge workers will be better educated. They will be specialists in their fields and will command higher salaries. Since they carry the companies' critical resource — knowledge — if they leave, a valuable commodity goes with them. The nature of their work will make them privy to much information. It will demand that they work in a self-directed mode with much autonomy. They will not as easily be replaced as service workers and will be highly valued. Perks may be considered as a method to attract and keep top-notch knowledge workers. They may be the ones occupying corner offices and pulling into private parking spots.

There is the danger that the knowledge workers may become the organization's new elite. The new organization cannot function with internal barriers and there is not time to knock down walls or build bridges. The potential division needs to be prevented.

People build resentment when others appear to be more appreciated than they. Perks and money are symbols of recognition and can be the focus of the resentment, but they are not the cause of resentment. We resent others, not because of their "good" treatment, but because of our perceived "poor" treatment.

Preventing divisiveness means ensuring that the basics are in place for a caring organization that creates an environment in which people can self-actualize:

- Full information sharing;
- Opportunities for personal growth;
- Shared leadership;
- Recognition of contributions (do not have to be monetary).

The caring organization is not one that makes people "feel" important but ensures people "know" they are important. When all workers feel good about themselves, they feel good about others and divisions don't occur.

## Organizational Tribalism

There is a potential for further divisions if the organization experiences tribalism. The globalism-tribalism polarity has emerged dramatically on the world stage. There are very few people in the world who have not felt the increasing global interconnectedness. In recent years we have seen political and economic walls come tumbling down in many parts of the world.

Being connected in an electronic world means no boundaries. Information flows freely. Everyone has access to the same common pool of information, not just international, political and economic news but sitcoms, music videos, soap operas and movies. As more businesses have global operations and markets are more easily accessed, products become increasingly common. People around the globe wear Levi's, eat Big Macs and talk about Princess Di and the British Royals' scandals. People from small villages in the Malaysian countryside to New Yorkers have many common frames of reference.

History is becoming global history and experiences are becoming global experiences. Not only did people around the world watch the war in Iraq, many of their countries participated. Economic swings in one part of the globe are felt directly or indirectly in another.

Common experiences, information and frames of reference accumulate to eventually develop a global culture. People experience a greater sense of commonality and oneness.

We are creating a homogeneous world. But the boundaries that have disappeared or have become blurred used to meet an important basic need. Most people cherish their uniqueness. The age-old question pondered since humans evolved into thinking beings — "Who am I?" — is always consciously or unconsciously being asked. The more homogeneous the world, the less obvious the answer on a cultural level. Boundaries create a sense of identity. As the sense of identity is lost in globalization, its opposite pole, tribalism, attempts to compensate. People try to parcel themselves with others of like kind into a smaller packet that they can understand and that has a certain uniqueness, which provides the required sense of identity and sense of belonging; hence Bosnians, Serbs,

Croatians and countless other groups around the globe insisting they be recognized as distinct.

Organizations have been experiencing their own globalization. Walls have come down, literally and figuratively. The organization has been flattened and wired; technology allows wide access to information and increases communication (remote offices that used to enjoy being beyond the prying eye of head office find that they are no longer invisible); cross-functional teams are removing old departmental barriers; many companies have opted for fewer offices and more open spaces; titles have disappeared (often even on business cards, everyone is an associate or partner); in some companies, associates introduce themselves outside of the company by name and company only, giving no title or even department or division. Shared values, shared leadership, teams and team rewards are the norm.

All of these changes represent a respect for all workers and a recognition of the importance of each one. Benefits have been reaped; for most, an increased sense of ownership, which translates into better customer service, quality, productivity and, in general, higher-caliber decisions and outcomes.

If, however, these new practices create too much commonality and diminish the sense of identity and belonging, the opposite pole, organizational tribalism, will emerge. People will cluster into groups of common interests, common causes or common thinking and will start building invisible walls that will break down the communication and the cohesiveness that are essential to the new organization. They may become activists and begin to lobby for their "rights."

Avoiding organizational tribalism requires:

• That the organization have a strong identity, not just a clear picture of the business it is in but who it is, including its history and strong corporate values of which members are proud;

• The sure knowledge for each member that he or she is making an important contribution, making him or her "part" of the organization. With this combination comes the sense of belonging and identity that people need. Members can say, "This is what I belong to." Organizations that can accomplish this will be highly valued. People who feel a loss of roots as a result of globalization can find the community they need in their organization.

# ATTRACTING AND KEEPING THE BEST

The new organization's success depends on its cumulative knowledge. Although expertise has always been crucial for business success, only a few employees were valued for their intellectual property. The rest contributed manual skills to the organization, perhaps by working on an assembly line or filing documents. The knowledge component of most jobs is quickly increasing, as are the number of jobs that qualify as knowledge work. Approximately two-thirds of workers are knowledge workers. Being the best in the business will mean having the best brains in the business. The ability to attract and keep the best knowledge will be the organization's edge.

In addition, the advantage of maintaining longer-term relations with all members who bring superior skills and commitment and who embrace the company's values will be strongly felt as organizations continue to hurtle through an unpredictable environment of change. Knowledge of others' strengths, and possible idiosyncrasies, allows team members to manage the unexpected and to quickly start up new teams. Individuals who have had a longer-term relationship with an organization have a stronger intuitive sense of who the organization is and what will work and what won't.

The traditional down side of employees working together for too long will not be a concern. The nature of the ever-evolving organization will require a regular injection of new people who will keep the longer-term members revitalized. People will be adept at looking at situations from new and different perspectives and will be skilled at examining and shifting their own paradigms. These abilities will be a basic requirement of the new organization.

Attracting and keeping the best will be a top priority for the organization. It is a priority that will reside with the executive group, and the company's annual track record for attracting and keeping the best, particularly knowledge workers, will be a key performance indicator.

## Providing a Quality Work Style

In the seventies and eighties, people worked primarily to maintain their lifestyle. This meant that money was a main motivator. As we move into a new millennium, we are seeing a significant change in personal values. People not only want their 7.5 or 10 hours a day to count for something, but want to balance their work life with the rest of their life. They want work to be a place or experience (since going to work no longer simply means heading for a particular building) that is compatible with their real self, not a self they put on to get through the work day. Work must allow them to be themselves and challenge them to be their best. People are searching for a work style that is one with their personal lifestyle.

Attracting and keeping the best will happen in organizations that fulfill these personal needs. What will organizations offer to meet these needs? Opportunities abound but there are indicators of some likely trends.

### Flexibility

Balancing personal life and work life has become a priority for most workers. Flextime will be an expectation.

The number of people working from home will continue to increase. It saves the company overhead costs, prevents office interruptions and so can increase productivity, and provides people for whom working at home works the ultimate flexibility. Some people, however, find that a home office doesn't work for them. There may be too many family interruptions or they may not enjoy working at home. For many, interactions in the workplace are a key component of their job satisfaction. Many companies now offer working at home as an option; in the future, many will probably offer working at the office as an option. For those working at home, there will likely be drop-in places where people can gather to exchange information and ideas or to just catch up, socially. Opportunity to interact personally will be provided by face-to-face meetings and other activities.

Companies that rank high on the "Preferred Employer" list — and in all likelihood there will be one — will demonstrate an understanding of the importance of the phrase John Naisbitt coined, "high tech, high touch." As people work in more separate environments in the new economy, they will have a greater need to connect, personally.

### Hire Me, Support My Family

Workers will be attracted to companies that provide family-oriented benefits. Average life spans will continue to increase and more people will be experiencing four-generation families. The adult income earners will be supporting their children and providing care for, if not financially supporting, parents and grandparents. There is room for plenty of creativity in the types of benefits offered, from child- and elder-care days off to on-site daycare for children and elders.

## The Important Things in Life

It is likely that time off will be highly valued even if it means less income. Workers who during the early nineties opted for shorter work weeks with less pay, rather than layoffs, found that even though their income was drastically cut, for the most part their quality of life went way up.

The preferred work style will include more casual dress. Casual Fridays (business casual) will be replaced by everyday casual. This will fit into the generally more casual lifestyle that most people will likely opt for and will reflect the increased merging of personal and work styles. It will also be seen as a cost saving — no need for both a business and casual wardrobe.

Systems and holistic thinking will apply globally, organizationally and personally. Over the past few years, a trend has been growing to develop ourselves spiritually and to search for more natural health treatments. People will be attracted to the organizations that best help them in their personal development and wellness, physically, emotionally and intellectually. Many companies already provide fitness facilities or club memberships. Some companies provide light early morning aerobics for teams in their workspace.

Time to still the mind will be accepted as essential to tap personal potential. It will also be used for stress reduction — there will be high performance expectations in the new organization. I do not know of statistics on the number of people who practice meditation and other relaxation techniques, but the percentage is high. As the walls between personal and work lives are broken down, and as companies search more for their own spirit, it is likely these personal practices will become organizational practices. We may see meditation breaks instead of coffee breaks, quiet or meditation rooms instead of coffee rooms, and more atriums or outdoor gardens with ponds or waterfalls, not just to walk by, but where people go to read or quietly relax.

Companies considered "good" places to work will make a strong commitment to supporting peoples' intellectual development. Life-long learning will be the norm and a requirement of good employment. Learning will occupy a good deal of time. Workers will look for organizations that will help them expand their knowledge base. Learning programs offered will include all of the areas that directly impact their performance, and are key in the new economy: communication, technology, teamwork and individual specialty areas. In addition, there will be a recognition that the panic to specialize and to emphasize the practical in order to find a place in the new economy has left many people without an education. There is a concern that the focus of "schooling" will be to get a job rather than to learn and that the new worker will not have the broad understanding of the arts and, in general, how the world works, which enriches one's understanding of problems and promotes creativity.

There is a danger that a vertical task focus is overtaking education. Task-focused education is a concern when we are living in a world that requires horizontal, process-oriented behaviors.

It is likely that the new organization will initially be heavily populated by specialists who are narrowly focused, but the need for workers who are more broadly educated will become evident. The broader the education, the easier it will be to make the essential links with other specialists and non-specialists; the broader the education, the less likely we are to get trapped in narrow paradigms that limit our perspectives and ability to solve problems; the broader our education, the greater the likelihood that we will be good environmental scanners, picking up the relevance of information that at first sight may seem to have little connection with the business we are in.

Companies that develop a reputation for the quality and variety of learning that they offer their members will have an advantage in attracting and keeping the best people. Specialists who also have a broad education will be in demand. Knowledge workers will need to broaden their education as part of the continuous learning to which everyone will be committed.

Much of the education now housed in academic institutions will move to the corporation. Companies are already providing learning that is recognized by university credits, for example, IBM's compulsory Virtual Team program. In addition, there may be learning programs on meditation or music appreciation.

Although the extra benefits will be important, ultimately an organization's ability to develop a sense of loyalty among its members will depend on the nature of the organization. It will be a caring organization that has high performance expectations of its members. Most important and most basic, the company will be one in which people are able to be themselves and bring out the best of themselves.

*The real act of discovery consists not in finding new lands, but in seeing with new eyes.*

Marcel Proust

Once settled in the new economy, the new organization will still face many of the same challenges we face today. Change will not go away, and if we choose to look for chaos and focus on it, there will still be chaos. The major difference will be that those organizations that have made it into the new economy will have learned how to work in an environment of change. They will be in sync with the larger system of which they are a part; they will be working with ease instead of struggling; they will be working within chaos rather than trying to control it. This sense of ease and oneness with the new world will be the result of new perspectives, looking at the old with new eyes. It will be the result of realizing that any struggle we experience is not created by the challenges we meet but by our reaction to them. The new organization will realize that it has the power to create its own reality, and will get busy and do it.

# BIBLIOGRAPHY

Alfred, Gerald R. *Heeding the Voices of Our Ancestors*. Toronto: Oxford University Press, 1995.

Chopra, Deepak. *Ageless Body, Timeless Mind*. New York: Harmony Books, 1993.

Dalla Costa, John. *Working Wisdom*. Toronto: Stoddart, 1995.

Davis, Stan, and Jim Botkin. *The Monster Under the Bed: How Business is Mastering the Opportunity of Knowledge for Profit*. New York: Simon & Schuster, 1994.

Drucker, Peter F. *Managing in A Time of Great Change*. New York: Truman Tally Books/Dutton, 1995.

Drucker, Peter F. *Post-Capitalist Society*. New York: HarperBusiness, 1993.

Forisha-Kovach, Barbara. *The Flexible Organization*. New Jersey: Prentice Hall, 1984.

Gates, Bill. *The Road Ahead*. New York: Viking Penguin, 1995.

Hammer, Michael. *Beyond Reengineering*. New York: HarperBusiness, 1996.

Hurst, David K. *Crisis & Renewal: Meeting the Challenge of Organizational Change*. Boston: Harvard Business School Press, 1995.

Jacques, Elliott. "In Praise of Hierarchy," *The Harvard Business Review*. Jan/Feb 1990.

Johnson, Barry. *Polarity Management*. Boston: H&D Press, 1992.

Mintzberg, Henry. *The Rise and Fall of Strategic Planning*. New York: The Free Press, 1994.

Ouchi, Thomas. *The Z Organization: How American Business Can Meet the Japanese Challenge*. New York: Addison-Wesley, 1981.

Phillips, Nikola. *From Vision to Beyond Teamwork: 10 Ways to Wake Up and Shake Up Your Company*. Burr Ridge, Il.: Irwin Professional Publishing, 1995.

Rowan, Roy. *The Intuitive Manager*. Boston: Little, Brown and Company, 1986.

Sankar, Yassin. *Value-Based Management for the Information Society: Some New Perspectives*. Toronto: Canadian Scholars' Press, 1991.

Schultz, Ron. *Unconventional Wisdom: twelve remarkable innovators tell how intuition can revolutionize decision-making*. New York: HarperBusiness, 1994.

Schwartz, Peter. *The Art of the Long View*. New York: Doubleday, 1991.

Senge, Peter M. *The Fifth Discipline*. New York: Doubleday, 1990.

Sharitz, Jay M., and J. Steven. *Classics of Organizational Theory*, 4th edition. New York: Harcourt Brace College Publishers, 1996.

Sinclair, Lister, with Robert Scott Root-Bernstein. *Exploring the Nature of Discovery*, Canadian Broadcasting Corporation, 1995. (radio program)

Toffler, Alvin, and Heidi Toffler. *Creating a New Civilization*. Atlanta, Ga.: Turner Publishing, 1994.

Watts, Alan. *Tao: The Watercourse Way*. New York: Pantheon, 1975.

Wilkstrom, Solveig, and Richard Normanson. *Knowledge and Value*. London: Routledge, 1994.

# INDEX

## A

Accepting individual differences, 140-143, 149
Accountability, 124, 127, 143-144, 169, 170
*Adaptive Corporation, The* (Toffler), 9
Age, and wisdom, 72-73
American Airlines, 3-4
AT&T, 9

## B

Balancing task and process, 15-18, 31-49, 73
  for effective leadership, 53-55
  individual, 48-49, 52-56
  in meetings, 42-48
  personal questionnaire, 56-67
  in teams, 36-49
  Yin and Yang of organization, 27-30
Baltes, Paul, 72
Banks, 111-112
Barker, Joel, 83
Beggs, Peter, 135
Benefits, employment, 179-180
Berrouard, Ross, 37
Big picture, 18, 52, 84, 92, 173
Bohr, Niels, 113
Broad education, 181
Butterfly effect, 6, 75

## C

Carey, Joe, 88
Caring organization, 165-66, 175-176, 179-181
Change
  Novice Effect, 84

organizational *see* New organization
  personal, 52-56
  rate of, 10-11, 16
Chaos theory, 6, 182
Commitment, 126-127
Communication
  among native people, 141, 142
  in large and virtual teams, 134-135, 136
  in vertical vs. horizontal organizations, 12-13
  *see also* Horizontal behavior; Vertical focus
Compartmentalized organization, 18, 97
Consensus, 11, 142-143, 149, 156
Continuous learning, 14-15, 51, 83, 88, 180-181
Convergent thinkers, 48, 54, 70
Craftsmanship, 161-163
Creative thinking, 51
Customer service, 77, 78
Customer-focused goals, 40, 88

## D

Dalla Costa, John, 72
Data, 3, 79
De Bono, Edward, 51
Decision-making process, 21, 23, 74-75
Demming, W. Edwards, 22
Dialogue, 11, 137-138, 146
Discussion, 137, 138
Dissipative structures, 15
Divergent thinkers, 51-52, 70
Divisiveness, preventing, 174-177
Dominance factor, 94
Drucker, Peter, 2, 50, 78, 171
Dunlop, Albert, 165

## E

e-mail, 90-91, 135
Early retirement, 73

# INDEX

# PRESENTATIONS BY LESLIE BENDALY

*Presentations range from one-hour keynote addresses to two-day workshops.*
- **Thriving in the New Economy**
  Essential Steps for Organizations
  Essential Steps for Individuals
- **The Next Corporate Challenge**
  Dealing with the Energy Shortage
- **Corporate Ethics**
  The Criteria for Success in the New Economy
- **Leadership for the New Economy**
  Beyond the Action Hero
- **Developing Organizational Wisdom**
- **Creating Teams That Work**
- **Beyond Reengineering**
  The Next Steps

**Other products and services available:**
- *Teamwork Essentials*
  A unique report — subscription includes right to copy
- Consulting on organizational change and developing high
  performance teams
- Team development workshops

**For speaking engagements contact:**
David Lavin Agency
Phone: (416) 979-7979 or 1-800-265-4870

**For workshops and other products and services contact:**
ORTRAN
Phone: (416) 440-0532
Fax: (416) 489-1173